*2005*

# This Is How I Did It:
# Nancy Kominsky

*The Struggle from Poverty
to Celebrity*

by
Nancy Kominsky

Third Edition
MetaMEDIA Communications
Drawer 28820
Bellingham WA 98228
http://www.metamediacom.tv
info@metamediacom.tv

Rev 3.3   April 30, 2009
ISBN-13:  978-0-578-02254-3

Designed by Michael A. Kominsky

# Contents

# Preface

I have decided to start with the flowers. They are the easiest for beginners.

Sitting in my Bristol hotel bedroom with tubes of oil paint before me, I squeeze lemon yellow, cadmium and yellow ochre—three tones, three colours for the sunflowers—on to the palette.

Then for the background, one teaspoonful of orange, half a teaspoonful of vermillion and half a teaspoonful of purple. I mix these background colours together and divide the mixture into three little heaps. To one I add half a teaspoonful of white; to the next, half a teaspoonful of vermillion, and to the last, half a teaspoonful of purple. Finally, I mix quarter of a teaspoonful of purple with the same amount of alizarin crimson.

Now I have the basic palette for my first television programme, *Paint Along With Nancy*.

I am nervous and excited because this is my dream coming true. HTV, based in Bristol have commissioned me to do a series of 13 how-to-paint programmes, using my own down to earth kitchen-sink system of teaching. There is no mystery, no arty language. Say "half a teaspoonful of white" and everyone knows how much you mean. As for the picture, I've got 26 minutes to do it from white canvas to finish.

I want to show everyone who watches how they can paint a picture just like mine using a method that cannot fail.

When the car comes to pick me up I have my paints and palette ready, and a roll of toilet paper to hang on the studio easel for wiping the palette knife. I have not got a script. It is all in my head.

* * *

We had coffee and biscuits in the television canteen, the two cameramen, the director and I, and then we went up to a big empty room where the corner was dressed up to look like an attic studio. The director asked me for a copy of my script so that he could direct the cameras and to his consternation I told him there wasn't one. I knew what I wanted to say. I had been wanting to say it for a long time.

I was wearing my smock. I hung the toilet roll on the easel, laid out the palette and some extra tubes of paint, propped up the canvas, lights flashed, they gave me the signal, and I began.

"We're going to start with flowers because they're the easiest," I said. "If you are painting carnations and someone says, 'Those are nice daisies', what does it matter? Just thank them and carry on." The aim was to paint a picture they could be proud of, a picture they could hang up. This was the school of no-failures.

Start painting a wash of umber on the canvas and dab it dry. Now paint a grid, three lines down, five across, then paint in the position of the flowers to get the composition right, exactly like this. I had to work fast. I only had 26 minutes.

I explained about mixing colours and tones, how to measure the amounts in teaspoons, told them to start with deciding where the light was coming from so that darker and lighter tones of the same colour defined the shapes. Paint in the background first, and if you make a mistake, scrape it off, which is easy with oil paints. I mixed quips with tips while laying on the paint at top speed, paints melting under the hot studio lights, and finished the picture, four open sunflowers and a bud, leaving just four minutes for wrapping up the programme credits and saying there'd be another *Paint Along With Nancy,* same time, same place next week.

Next day the letters started to come in, a flood of fan mail. So that was the start of what became several series of paint-along programmes that sold on to European and Asian countries and to the US.

How did it all begin? No one watching could have guessed at the miserable poverty and hunger of my childhood in America, the betrayals and abuse, the struggle to hold off disaster, endless scrounging just to live, the terrible loss that still brings tears to my eyes, and the love and friendships that helped me fight back and win.

Friends ask, "How did you do it?"  I did it because they helped me. So I wrote a book to tell them: This Is How I Did It.

# Acknowledgement

I would like to thank my husband Patrick Wodehouse for all his support and patience, my son Michael, my daughter Nancy, and Sebastian Thomas for his artistic contributions.

My very special thanks and love to Yvonne Thomas.

# Chapter 1

It was early in the morning and the noise began like an explosion. It travelled like fire across the city of Philadelphia and by the time it had reached our street it had risen to a huge, shrieking crescendo, with people blowing whistles and shouting, women running from the houses still wearing their pinnies, banging cooking pots together, singing and dancing on the sidewalks and into the road. Firemen played their hoses up to the sky so that the water fell glittering like fountains and everybody was laughing and cheering for the news had just come through.

The war had ENDED!

It was the eleventh of November 1918.

This is my first memory.

I am the three year-old girl sitting on the doorstep of a terraced house in Hicks Street, which is in Philadelphia's Little Italy close to the lively Italian market. It is not a smart area but it is respectable. And even if a neighbour does not know my name which is Emanuella Circelli, they can see I have Italian parents because of the big brown eyes and dark hair just like most of the other bambinos down the street.

I can tell this is a big day, not only because of the noise, but because my mother, who is so smart—too smart for the rest of the street, and who usually keeps herself to herself has come out into the road as well, laughing and banging a pan like the rest of them, joining in the fun and gets wet under the firemen's fountains without minding.

In the house a few doors down where the Crenellis lived, the old lady died as the armistice was announced and the priest who arrived to give her the last rites comes out with his little white bag, raises his arms to stop the din and tells us we must all pray. Everyone, including me, kneels in the street and thanks God that the war has ended.

Next day, the Philadelphia Inquirer, which is our local newspaper, described every minute of that first wild celebration of peace in the city streets. "Business Stops While Every Man, Woman and Child Joins In Rejoicing"…"Early Morning Whistles Carry News Of Victory To Sleepers" the headlines go. And below, the reports: "The first consciousness of victory broke but slowly upon the slumbering people of the city. In the black hours, long before dawn, the sleepers awoke and heard it—the mighty chorus of whistles, penetrated by the sharp crack of small arms, the deep boom of canon, the harsh note of the tin horns and the clangour of bells from every spire and steeple."

These descriptions by long-departed reporters confirm that vivid cameo of sound and colour in my distant memory. Now I can read that "from three in the morning" (the time distance from Europe) "throughout the thirteen hours till midnight, the lowly and the poor, in stately mansions of the rich, the city marched and sang and lifted up its soul and rejoiced."

The crowds streamed along the streets to Independence Hall and the "great golden statue of liberty at the South Plaza of the City", others waving from the windows of the packed hotels which were open till 4am by mayoral decree. The governor-elect's son who had been gassed in France led the procession and as the brass band marched, tears ran down the players' cheeks. The Mayor declared a holiday and said the rejoicing would make the celebrations after the Spanish-American war seem like a village carnival; gun-happy celebrators accidentally shot a few people, some fatally, and the Home Defense Reserve had to come out to help the police keep order.

What I remember best is that after all this rejoicing my father came home. How handsome he was in his army uniform, tall with thick wavy hair, laughing and joking with his friends. He looked and acted like a wartime hero though in fact he had not left the shores of the United States because the war ended before his draft was sent out. But he had had time to get lots of photographs of himself looking glamorous in khaki and he had such stories to tell about the war, he was the most exciting hero in our neighbourhood.

The pretty girls he flirted with believed it all. And so did I, as he swept me up and kissed me and called me his little dreamer.

After the war we settled down to the Peace. But not to a peaceful routine, because nothing in our house was peaceful or routine. That would have been impossible with parents like ours.

Still, the family expanded like most of the other Italian families in our neighbourhood at the beginning of the century, and eventually I had three little sisters and a brother who added to the noisy clamour of our street. Golden-haired Maria was born 16 months after me. Then Leonard, our only brother, who looked like an angel with his blond curls and blue eyes, one lighter than the other. Mother, whose hair was dark with auburn lights said that his colouring must have come from her side because her family was from northern Italy near the Swiss border where there are a lot of blond Italians.

I adored Leonard. Though he was five years younger than me he was my chief ally in the terrible years to come, doing his best to take on responsibilities like a man before he was killed while still a child.

For the next few years before the two youngest were born, we five lived in the small terraced house that looked exactly like all the other small terraced houses in Hicks Street and like all the other houses across the cobbled road.

I remember few neighbours who were not Italian. There was a big influx of immigrants from Italy to Philadelphia at the beginning of the century, mainly peasant people and many of them really only wanted to stay long enough to earn the price of a few acres of land in the old country so that they could go back home and farm it.

Meanwhile, in this foreign city of Philadelphia they strove to make life as much as possible as it was in the place they had left behind.

The Italian market, now a famous attraction of the town down 9th Street was the centre for gossip and trade and we Italians lived around it. We all went to the market to buy fruit and vegetables, home-made cheese, home-brewed wine, fresh spaghetti and olive oil sent from Italy, even live animals for slaughter, and it was the hub of our community.

Life was far from quiet. Put a crowd of Italians together and one thing you do not get is silence. My early memories are of ceaseless noise, screaming children, their clogs clattering on the stones, mothers outside scrubbing the five marble steps up to their houses and polishing the brass doorknobs, shouting gossip to each other and yelling at the children.

I also remember the summer noises. The rattle of the horse pulling the ice-man's wagon down the street, clip-clop over the cobbles. My mother would run out with a huge pan to buy a block of ice, and put it in the cellar to make it last. Even more exciting was the sound of the ice-cream man's bell, which he rang to announce his coming as he pushed a cart with big rickety wheels down the middle of the road.

His barrow had a red and white striped awning and we all knew what he kept under it. A huge block of ice cream, packed around with ice, and rows of flavours in bottles. He used to scrape a dollop off the block and shake on the flavour you pointed to, bright green, or crimson, or gold, then ring his bell and with a shove, start the big wheels rolling on. Sometimes on Saturdays, when it was very hot and you could feel the stones underfoot baking through your shoes, the police turned on the fire hydrants down the street, and all of us children ran out in our underclothes or naked but for a vest and danced about under the jets of water.

If you were out in the summer evening you could smell the aroma of cooking mingling from the houses as other mothers, like my own, put the spaghetti on the little stoves with the garlic and tomatoes and sometimes a sizzling steak. I missed all that when we moved to a better area.

The narrow street was lit with gas and the lamplighter came in the dusk with his long pole and a flame flickering at the tip to light the mantles. And as the neighbourhood grew quieter for the evening, the greenish-yellow gaslight shone from the windows (nobody of course had electricity). You could still hear the sounds of the city: the trolley cars clanging where the rails intersected by the main street, and the muffled sound of fog horns coming up from the big merchant ships at the docks on the Schuylkill River.

When I was older I used to go down to that river. I would gaze at the ghostly ships with the foreign flags and mysterious destinations, and dream of one day sailing away from Philadelphia to the great, exciting, wonderful world outside

# Chapter 2

Although we were happy in Hicks Street there was never much question of us staying there because my father had bigger ideas.

He wasn't like the other fathers in the street. He was going somewhere else. Upward. He looked the part, and he acted it. Other men could wear baggy trousers and scuffed shoes and trail off to the market on Saturday morning where all good Italians bargained for vino, cheese and vegetables. Not him.

He was always immaculate: the suit well-pressed, shirt collar white and stiff with starch, the tie quiet but expensive. I can see him now in his fedora hat, the familiar white carnation in his buttonhole, jaunty and smiling, greeting friends on all sides. Father was gregarious and he loved dressing up. He never wore anything cheap or flashy: he had style. All he wanted was the best that money could buy. No one was sure where his money came from but you could see right away that for him quality counted.

"Here comes a person of status and taste", his appearance proclaimed. Appearances can be misleading but if you want to get on you had better look the part, and for father that came as naturally as the sun rising in the morning.

Looking back I recognise a man with charisma, a confident, swashbuckling personality attractive to men as well as women. Witty and amusing, a good raconteur, in love with life and all the best it could offer, there was always much laughter and back-slapping in his company and of course the ladies (he loved them all) responded richly to his charm and attention.

Six months after the war had ended, father was on his way. He was a businessman, an entrepreneur, a future millionaire and we flourished in the warmth of his self-assurance and optimism. It was a golden time when we felt secure and happy; a time when we expected everything to go right forever.

You take things at face value when you are a child. Though even then I, as the eldest, could feel some undercurrents of friction at home because my tall, beautiful mother was exactly the opposite to the man she married. As much as he loved to be the centre of a group of noisy friends, she hated it. And there was the recurring question: where is the money coming from?

Little did I care about that. I just remember him buying me beautiful dolls with long hair I could comb, and eyes that opened and shut and clothes that came off. The local newspaper carried adverts, "Dolls at $1.40 each, made in Japan (but with pretty American baby faces)" alongside leaders that kicked off with assertions like, "Truth to tell, no German can be trusted"— and post-war normality returning, we settled down to security and prosperity.

Father liked being married. He was proud of his children—only three of us yet. Every Sunday he marched us down the narrow cobbled street to Broad Street, which was much smarter than ours—and the brownstone house where his mother lived. My mother always refused to go too, but she made sure we were turned out smartly.

Marie and I had fur hats and coats trimmed with matching rabbit fur and wore shiny patent leather shoes called Mary-Janes with a strap across the instep, and white lawn stockings which mother made and folded away in drawers with bags of lavender. My brother Leonard was tall for his age and full of mischief, but on our visits with father we behaved as well brought-up children should: excited but very polite.

"Where's Tessie?" grandmother used to ask, as if she expected my mother to have come too, though she must have known that mother hated going anywhere. It must have hurt her feelings, for Michael was her only son. On the other hand, he had done rather well in the marital stakes because his wife Theresa had looks and breeding and he had snatched her in the teeth of her well-off family's opposition.

What was just as important in those days, she was third generation American, and the Circelli family, grandmother Emanuella after whom I was named and her husband Leonardo were newcomers.

In the 1920s, new Italian immigrants in Philadelphia were socially at the bottom of the heap and most of them were employed in the labouring and sweatshop jobs.

My father Michael was an infant in arms when his parents stepped ashore at Ellis Island with two little sisters, Josephine and Rose in tow, and like so many Italian immigrants before and since, the family made their way down to Philadelphia, the city of promise and hope, if not exactly of brotherly love.

Before they emigrated my grandfather had been a farm worker in the south. It must have been a hard life to drive him from his native land, the sunshine and gentle slopes of the vineyards from which he made enough rich red wine for the family.

But Leonardo was a practical man, and now in the land where anyone who worked hard could make a fortune it made sense for his son to learn a trade. So when young Michael left school, his father apprenticed him to a barber.

Obediently my father donned a white apron, swept up shorn hair and started learning how to deliver short back and sides to the clients. Then Leonardo, who wished to set up his smart son with a job for life bought him a barber's shop in a good part of the town near the station. However this was not really how father saw his future. It was too slow.

He was still in his teens and looking for ways to raise the horizons when he found what could be a good start. He met a sweet young Jewish girl. She was only 19. And she had a rich father.

Knowing my father's affection for women I am sure he fell in love with her, as she certainly did with him. However, father knew enough about the world to realise that cutting hair was not a job that carried much status or glamour. It was not like, for instance, being an idealistic young medical student. So, why not *be* a medical student?

At least he could look like one. He got hold of some text books, carried them round everywhere, read up about diseases, treatments, medicines and spoke about healing the sick like a young man heading for sainthood. The girl was head over heels. Her father was not.

You don't get to being a rich businessman by believing anything you are told, and the Jewish papa was not going to watch an Italian, of all people, making off with his only child and heiress.

"But he's a medical student," his daughter pleaded. "Won't you just meet him?"

Young Michael Circelli was invited to dinner with the family and because he was so busy, always dashing off to lectures and vivas he arrived with medical books tucked under his arm, and set about winning them over. He was handsome, amusing with a ready wit and spoke knowledgeably about medicine—and even if he was Italian, he would some day be a doctor...Yet, the old Jew thought, could he be after the money?

His daughter knew otherwise. It was true love. And yes, she was ready to elope. So that was what they did: ran away to marry and moved to cheap rented rooms, from which Michael went every day, medical books under his arm, to the barber's shop.

They were happy and the weeks went by without incident until Michael had some rotten luck. Though it is difficult to work out what he had in mind for the future, the medical-student myth was working perfectly until his wife's father had to take a business trip, and before getting on the train he nipped into the barber's shop by the railway station and beheld his son-in-law, the barber. He was horrified and furious.

He moved fast. He went to the law. His daughter had been under age, she had been deceived: he demanded an annulment and he got it. The marriage had lasted a few months.

My father was not one to be laid low for long, and there were other pretty girls to be wooed and won. There was, for instance, that tall, auburn-haired beauty, Theresa Lauria who lived in Montrose, one of the smarter streets in Little Italy.

Theresa had an elder sister called Rose and two brothers Louis and Michael, and they all played musical instruments and lived a genteel life as befitted a third generation family with a fortune behind it.

Theresa was very shy and retiring, but if anyone could quicken the interest of a timid girl and charm her into his orbit, it was Michael Circelli.

# Chapter 3

Mother's grandfather, Nicholas had come over from Italy as a teenage carpenter and made the family fortune: not a lavish one, but a good foundation that enabled his children and grandchildren to be well educated and live comfortably. Many years later, as my own childhood slid into fear and poverty I used to think of him. For his survival was a miracle, like a signal down the years that we would also survive.

Until he was 15 he had lived with his parents and numerous brothers and sisters in Messina on the northern tip of Sicily. Sheer luck saved his life. His father who was a poor farmer wanted all his sons to learn a trade, and Nicolo was sent to be apprenticed to his cousin, a carpenter in the neighbouring village. The very next day after he left there was a terrible earthquake that destroyed much of Messina, and his entire family perished, save for one brother who was also away at the time.

There was nothing left for them in Italy, so at the age of 16 and with hardly any money, great grandfather wrote asking a cousin who had already migrated to Philadelphia to sponsor him and guarantee him a job in America. His surviving brother came too, but decided to try his luck further south and disappeared from family view in Argentina. We never knew what happened to him.

Meanwhile, Nicolo, who quickly became 'Nicholas', was met by his cousin's family. The sea journey he described to them was of terrible discomfort, death, sickness, probably the same story repeated on every immigration boat with crowded decks, people crammed into steerage, women giving birth on deck, compulsory physical examinations to check the spread of disease—and at last, the statue of liberty which they all cheered as the ship came in to dock.

Nicholas was a short, blond teenager. He had been brought up to a hard life and he knew it would not be easy, but he also knew where he was going. His cousin gave him temporary lodging and went with him next day to buy some carpentry tools on which Nicholas spent his last money. Then he was ready for work.

His first job was as a hired labourer doing repairs in private houses in Philadelphia, where many of them were made of wood. There was plenty of work for carpenters willing to work hard and for long hours and it did not take long for Nicholas to be making enough to put some aside after paying his keep. As soon as he had a little nest egg he put it down as a deposit on one of the derelict early 19th century houses in the old part of the town, and moved in.

Nobody wanted to live there. The area was in decay.

"The people who had last inhabited them were poor and they couldn't afford to do the repairs," old Nicholas used to tell his family, four tall blond boys all in professions and a brood of grandchildren. "The houses were built nearly entirely of wood, so you see how lucky I was that my father insisted on my training to be a carpenter. I renovated one house while I lived in it, then I rented it out and used the money to move to the house next door, and did the same again."

Bit by bit, great grandfather worked his way to a good, solid fortune. I sometimes think that but for people like him, those houses which are now on Philadelphia's tourist map in the old part of town could have been left to deteriorate until the site was cleared for redevelopment and part of our history would have been lost.

At the time of course, nobody thought like that. What his children and grandchildren most wanted to hear about was the treasure he found, left behind or lost by former occupants before they moved on. There was nothing really valuable; some coins from the early 1800s, a few clay churchwarden pipes, the bowls singed from tobacco and the stems well-chewed, bits of lace and things that today would be called antiques, but then were considered rubbish.

Typically of a self-made man, Nicholas wanted all his children to have the best education he could buy. He insisted on the five of them playing a musical instrument: his daughter Rose, my grandfather, Joseph who became a professional violinist and three other sons who went to universities, one emerging as a doctor, one a dentist and the third, a pharmacist. Then he set up a trust to ensure their children were also well educated.

Joseph married another Italian, Mary, who became my dear strong-minded grandmother, an ally in adversity, and long before the world followed, a believer in women's rights and education. While grandfather and his violin starred in concerts and orchestras, Mary brought up their four children, Rose, Mary, Nicholas, and the youngest, my mother Theresa.

Everyone said Theresa was especially pretty. Some of the neighbours used to call her "the belle of Montrose"—the street where they lived three blocks away from the port—and she was accomplished, too. Following the family tradition, she learned to play a musical instrument, in her case, the piano. She was also an excellent seamstress and when we were children she hand-made all our underclothes of the finest lawn, trimming them with lace, and our dresses, folding them away with lavender to keep them fresh and free from moths. She was elegant, and shy—more reticent than most young women of her age and breeding, maybe because she had suffered from a calcium deficiency in her late teens, which made her legs bowed, and she had to wear heavy braces to straighten them.

By the time she met my father she had long discarded them, but not, perhaps, the self-consciousness that teenagers can suffer at the best of times. Yet she had a lovely complexion, richly coloured hair lit by red lights, and a cultured family background.

This was the woman my father set his sights upon. They met at the Firemen's Ball. My grandmother was not at all pleased. What she saw was a divorcee—never a welcome suitor in a catholic home—and one moreover who had cruelly conned his innocent young wife and had a reputation as a womaniser. What's more, he was merely a barber, first generation at that.

What my mother saw was a handsome young man with thick, wavy chestnut hair, dark eyes, aged 21 like herself but full of charm, ease of manner and confidence that made even her shyness disappear. She fell in love with him. And when he asked her to marry him, she said 'Yes'.

Her mother however said 'No', and went one further.

She visited the priest of the catholic church of St Mary Magdalene opposite their house, and told the fellow—whom she had never much liked—that he was not to perform a marriage service for her daughter.

God's earthly representative was wise enough to agree.

My grandmother had an alternative suitor in mind for her youngest and fairest child: a quiet, serious-minded lawyer, attractive enough though a little shorter than my mother, and in love with her. She had as good as arranged it. But no, my mother had made up her mind.

Her father's three brothers, the doctor, the dentist and the pharmacist had a family meeting and begged her to reconsider. No, mother's mind would not be changed. And as Father Antonio Isoleri would not marry her, even though grandmother had been feuding with him for years, she ran away to her Aunt Rose.

She told Rose, "If you don't take me in, I'll walk into the river till my hat floats." With a threat like that, what could Aunt

Rose do? "And I'll run away with him and not get married," mother said to clinch it.

"Oh, no you won't. You'll have a proper wedding, and from my house," declared Aunt Rose, and that is what happened. Rose provided the dress, the reception, and my grandmother never forgave her.

I have a photograph of the wedding group: father sanding behind his bride, stiff in his white starched shirt, a carnation in his buttonhole , staring unsmiling ahead; his two sisters and Aunt Rose in their maid-of-honour finery. Looking at the bride, with her huge bouquet, silk gown overlaid with lace, and pensive face framed by a flower-decked cloche hat, one can only be thankful that the future is hidden from us.

# Chapter 4

The triumphant young lovers moved to Hicks Street. All the houses stood in a row looking exactly like their neighbours from the outside: five marble steps up to the front door, a brass knocker that needed polishing every day, a stout door, rarely locked or even shut in summer, and four windows facing the narrow cobbled road.

Michael put down a deposit, and it was theirs. It was nothing like as grand as the home Theresa had run away from, but now defiantly happy and untypically optimistic, Mrs Circelli set about improving the standards.

This was a crowded working-class area where the neighbours all knew each other, gossiped about each other's business, their children played and shouted together in the street and on Sundays the fathers strutted like proud, burnished cockerels showing off their families.

It was a friendly community. But my mother did not have friends. These people, newcomer "greenhorn" Italians—were her social inferiors and she did not care to socialise anyway. She had plenty to do in the house; she loved pretty things and her husband enjoyed buying them for her. For the moment she was content.

She quickly had babies. First: me, then Marie, and when the hero in battledress returned after the war, Leonard was born.

The house was too small for the growing family but we managed. There were just three rooms on the ground floor: the parlour, which was the best room where mother kept her Lester piano (father who admired mother's musical talent said he paid $1,000 for it but he usually exaggerated), then there was the dining room, and at the back was the kitchen with a mock-marble linoleum floor.

A little sunroom had been added to the kitchen as an extension and it led to a small yard enclosed by a five-foot wooden fence. Mother used to hang clothes out to dry in the yard, and there was just enough room around the edge to have a little border of herbs, without which no Italian food is complete.

Upstairs were two bedrooms and a little bathroom with running water and a proper flushing lavatory.

There was another space: I never thought of it as a room exactly. In the entrance hall of the house was a bolted door and when you opened it you could see wooden steps descending into darkness. This was the cellar. It had a dirt floor into which I once planted water melon seeds. They germinated quickly, grew to about two inches looking sickly and yellow for want of light, then flopped over and died.

Some of our neighbours—and my grandfather Joseph, too—kept barrels of maturing wine in their cellars. They made it themselves just as they had in the land of their birth from grapes tasted and selected with an experienced eye from the Italian market.

Grandfather sometimes took me with him to the market when the grapes came in. You could feel the excitement: wooden stalls with vats of olives, every cheese you could think of, sheep's, goat, buffalo, cow's; piles of vegetables and flowers as colourful as a Renoir painting. And the sounds: customers and vendors, neighbours and children calling out to each other, shouts and greetings vying with the bleating of goats, clucking hens, and the mingling of smells…

The grapes would be in huge boxes, lining the streets and customers pulled them out to taste them.

Grandfather held some up, ate one from a box and moved on to another. He plucked a few more and handed one to me to taste. When he was satisfied that he had the right quality, he would buy a few boxes and order them to be delivered at his house where he had grape presses in the basement, and all the barrels on trestles around the wall. He loved his wine. He made red and white.

Father was more imaginative in his use of the cellar but like many of the immigrants around us he sometimes acted as if we were in an Italian rural village.

Not so my mother. She liked clothes, soft kid gloves, and fashionable shoes. And father indulged her, for he liked fine things too. He wanted to show her off, and he was proud to be a cut above the neighbours with the wife he possessed as well as the things he bought. When mother admired expensive china, he bought it for her. She wanted the best lace curtains for the dining room, so he bought them, too. Above the large round dining table hung a tiffany lampshade, the latest in interior chic, and I remember a long, imposing sideboard against the wall.

The sitting room had two lots of curtains: lace, and then heavy velour drapes that were reversible, dark red and blue. Mother used to change them round to suit her mood. As well as the piano there was a settee and two armchairs and my mother's collection of Wallace Nutting watercolour prints of the Pennsylvania countryside.

None of the houses had electricity at this time. Ours was lit by gas and the kitchen had a little gas stove with a wire grill into which you could put a steak and hold it over the flames to singe. Father liked his steaks cooked in this way. It is one of the smells I associate with Hicks Street: fat dripping onto fire, spitting, burning and making thin trails of greasy smoke mingled with the appetising aroma of sizzling beef.

There is another that sends my memory back over the decades more vividly than any photograph. It is the whiff of singeing hair. I am there, with my mother, watching her use the curling tongs to coax her long tresses into the latest fashionable style, a daily part of her toilet, which was never neglected.

I see her first holding the tongs in the fire, and then she tests them on a piece of paper till they no longer scorch it. You have to watch out—there are plenty of stories about women who burned their hair right off by being careless. It is the sort of thing you read about in women's magazines. When the tongs are just right, mother deftly applies the blades to curl up the ends of her hair and as she does so, the acrid smell of singeing reaches my nostrils and hangs about in the air.

The next stage is to stuff a little pad of false hair called a rat under her own at the back of the crown to give more height (she was tall for a woman as it was—five-foot seven) then she rolls up the rest into a long sausage around her head and secures it with hairpins. I watch in silent admiration, my own dark hair cut in a bob with a fringe, straight and without a hint of a curl.

Whenever mother went out, she perched a little hat on top of her head. She had a collection of pretty hats, all the latest fashion and neatly stacked in boxes with tissue paper, for mother was a meticulous housekeeper and fastidious about her appearance.

Around the house she usually wore a little white lace or plain cotton blouse caught at the waist and a serge skirt, always with an apron over it. I remember her pointed shoes with bows on them and little heels and liked to try them on and shuffle around the room when she was not looking.

While other mothers laughed and gossiped in the street and father was out with his business associates pursuing some mysterious work that brought in lots of money, our mother would be playing the piano or tidying the house or at her sewing machine. She made stockings and underwear for herself and her children out of lawn and trimmed it with lace; dresses of organdie with ruffles round the skirt for my sisters and me, and breeches and little matching jackets for Leonard. As a housekeeper you couldn't fault her. But as a wife and mother, that was another matter.

I do not remember her being affectionate: she was too reserved. And yet she had been passionate about father, and run away to marry him. And yet again...even as a small child I sensed something wrong. They were of course, mismatched, but there was more to it than that.

Outside our house stood a modern wonder, the talk and envy of the neighbourhood: a red, open-top touring automobile. It had big brass lamps in front, and father said it was the only one that also had a brass light at the side on the running board so that we could see where to step up. People used to stop to admire it, smooth their hands over the shining red bonnet and speculate about what it had cost. When Leonard was five years old he climbed in and took the brake off and as the car started rolling away father came roaring out of the house just in time to leap aboard and stop it.

Marie, Leonard and I used to feel proud and excited sitting in a row at the back with father driving and mother beside him. Every journey was an adventure, for father was a terrible driver. It was the days before driving tests: you simply bought the thing and roared off in it.

Temperamentally, father should not have been in charge of a wheelbarrow, let alone the most powerful thing yet invented on four wheels. He shouted at us, at pedestrians who wandered into the road, he gleefully put his foot down on the accelerator to demonstrate his prowess and the brass needle moved up to a terrifying 20 miles and hour. Father enjoyed it all.

Mother, true to her nature, was uneasy with such flamboyance. She enjoyed the clothes father bought her, the jewellery, the piano, elegant suits, four fur coats and the best fittings money could buy for the house but when she asked him about the mysterious business that brought in such luxuries he was vague and evasive. Did all this come from the barber's shop?

The gossips in the Italian sector—and there were plenty of them—hinted that it did not.

One day he bought her a musquash coat, the fashionable fur of the 'twenties. I held it to my face to feel its softness, rippled my fingers through the chestnut-coloured hairs so that they caught the sun and glittered.

"Isn't it beautiful, mother!" I said.

"It doesn't suit me," she said, and fetched the scissors. "It makes me look old. I don't like the colour."

Snip, snip, she cut it up, unpicked the sleeves, laid out the bits. She was going to sew it up in a different style, but expert seamstress as she was, it was beyond her.

Father was furious. He shouted at her, she was defiant; he went out of the house slamming the door. He had friends, and some of them were women. He did not come back for a week.

Mother tightened her lips, lifted her chin and with silent anger cleaned and tidied as usual. She was too proud to say anything, and anyway there was no one to confide in as the marriage, which had started with such headstrong love and romance, slid relentlessly downhill.

# Chapter 5

Whatever Michael's failings as an upright husband, he was never dull. His rows were terrible and noisy; he was flamboyant and unreliable, a chancer, but he was an indulgent father.

On summer week ends, when the ice cream man came by he would send me out to buy five cones, one each, and I'd come skipping home hardly able to hold them with the ice cream dripping down my hand, and he relished the domesticity of our lives.

One day he told me, "You can go and buy the groceries today." He wrote, "Eggs, lettuce, tomatoes" on the list , gave it to me with a dollar bill and off I wandered, feeling big and responsible to our local shop. I glanced at the list. I could easily remember what was on it, so I threw it away. At the shop I ordered the goods and drew out the dollar to pay. But it wasn't the dollar. It was the list, and I had thrown the money away.

I went home empty-handed and confessed. Some fathers might have laughed, or given a mild rebuke. Not he. Father was furious. He shouted and yelled at me, his face red with anger and his eyes flashing. I should have been used to it because he shouted a lot, whenever anything annoyed him, which was often. It would pass, but leave us trembling. Somehow one never got used to my father's roaring angers, though my mother would stay icily silent.

Increasingly she showed her disapproval, especially when father came home with expensive gifts for us, like beautiful china dolls with eyes that opened and shut and real curly hair for Marie and me and a tricycle that looked like a motorbike with a sidecar for Leonard. When we played in the street with the neighbourhood children, we looked like the rich kids on the block, and it caused comment.

Mother's disapproval was becoming more a feature of our daily life. Father just carried on being himself: exuberant, enthusiastic, always with friends, some of whom did not look the sort of people grandmother would have welcomed to tea. And always, he had brilliant ideas.

One year he decided we should celebrate Easter in the traditional Italian way. He loved holidays and he didn't mind splashing out on them—as he didn't mind splashing out on anything. So Leonard and I went with him to the market on 9$^{th}$ Street to do the shopping.

At certain times of the year the Italian market expanded with a small pen for livestock. It would contain tethered goats, maybe some chickens and rabbits to be fattened up and butchered by the customer as was the tradition in Italy for festive occasions. What was practical in rural Italy was not at all practical in a crowded American city but that did not put father off in the slightest.

He bought a billy goat. It was a kid, a pretty little thing with a soft pink tongue, yellow eyes, horns, and a lot of young strength. Leonard and I stroked him, fed him some cabbage leaves while father paid then we led him off home at the end of a rope. My father's plan was to fatten him up in the yard for Easter. My mother, three generations removed from rural Italy was horrified.

"You can't put him there. That's where I hang out the washing. He'll eat the herb garden…"

She could protest all she liked. When father had an idea he liked to carry it out. But the goat decided things by butting so furiously at the wooden fence surrounding the yard that the neighbours complained.

Undaunted, father led him into the house, unbolted the door in the hall, and persuaded the reluctant animal to descend the wooden steps down to the cellar.

Because the house was so small and pokey my mother used the cellar for storing big pots and pans, which she hung along the walls. The goat did not like being down there. He charged against the pots and pans making a terrible racket, then he bounded up and down the wooden steps and butted against the door. It was a din to wake the dead. Mother was terrified. She was certainly not going to open the cellar door to feed the animal.

"What's the matter with you?" roared my father. "It's not going to hurt you!" Leonard and I cowered with my mother. It was like having the devil in a biscuit tin. "He has to be fed," shouted father. "We are fattening him not starving him to death!"

"But Daddy, he charges," we said. Father didn't want to know. The goat made such a din that after a few days the neighbours called the police.

The Law demanded entry, strutted into the hallway, observed the quivering cellar door as the poor kid crashed his embryo horns into the wood, and bravely drew the bolts.

"This is my property. You've no right…" father was shouting.

"You're disturbing the peace," the policemen yelled back at him.

Out of the cellar shot the kid. The Law snatched at the rope round the animal's neck and led the frightened creature out, still bucking and charging. That was the last we saw of our traditional Easter feast.

It would have been far less trouble if father had just made wine and stored it in barrels in the cellar like his neighbours, but no: if he could not have a goat, he would get some other animal to fatten. A rabbit. He brought one home in a basket.

"He won't make any noise. He's very quiet," father said. "The children will like him."

He was right. The children loved him. The rabbit was fluffy and trusting. He lolloped over and we stroked and petted him and hand fed him corn and greens from the kitchen. He had fawn-coloured fur, brown eyes and a little white tail and was far more loveable than a china doll. He grew plump and tame and confident of our affection.

At Easter, father declared, "It's time to get the rabbit."

"But Daddy!" We were speechless with horror.

Father took a knife and went down the cellar steps. Leonard, Marie and I ran to the door at the top, crying and screaming, "No, Daddy! No, Daddy!" We were filled with terror. He couldn't mean to kill our gentle little pet. But he did.

We made such a fuss and noise, father cut his own hand, which only made him angrier. He grabbed the rabbit and killed it. We all wept and wailed as he gutted and skinned it, his hands bloody, and then he shoved the warm, limp corps into my mother's hands and ordered, "Cook it." Father was in one of his rages. Reluctantly my mother cooked the rabbit, put it on a plate, and crying, we sat around the table while father cut it into joints.

We all had a piece of our pet before us.

"Eat it," shouted father. But we couldn't. We sat there crying, and my mother said angrily to him, "You must be crazy."

Next day we were silent and shocked. Father knew he had gone too far and he tried to make it up to us by buying things. But I think mother was right. Sometime his impatience and sudden anger made him lose all sense. Then the sun would come out again and with equal impatience he expected us to settle back to normality—as far as that word could ever be used in our house. For life with father was never normal.

As Christmas drew near he decided we should have the traditional Italian Christmas Eve delicacy, a plateful of eels. Without saying anything about it to mother, he went to market carrying a big pot with a lid, had it filled with eels and brought them home. He did not show them to mother: he just put the pot down and said, "There's a pile of eels here. I want you to cook them for the holidays. They won't hurt you—just pour boiling water on them." Then he strode out to attend to his business.

Mother lit the gas stove ready to cook the eels. She took the lid off the pot and they all came slithering out, onto the floor, black slimy things that moved so fast you'd have a job catching them—not that anyone tried. Mother started screaming hysterically and stood on a chair. Her shrieks were so loud, that the neighbours came tearing in.

They were first generation Italians: they were used to eels for Christmas Eve. They picked them up, put them back in the pot, calmed down mother and made her a cup of coffee.

"Just pour boiling water over them," explained one of the women. Mother looked as if she would faint. "Here, we'll do it." The neighbour boiled the kettle, gingerly lifted the lid of the pot, and poured in a torrent of boiling water. The poor eels subsided.

When father came back for lunch, mother tipped the pot onto a plate and the eels lay there twitching. We sat around the dining table—mother was very fussy about good table manners—awaiting the treat with dread, for we had heard the commotion from the kitchen.

The eels twitched. "Daddy," we screamed, "they're moving. Look! They're moving! They're alive."

"Eat it!" roared my father, taking one himself and slashing it with his knife. "Go on! Eat it!" He stuffed a forkful into his mouth and we watched with awe and horror but no one would follow. Father's temper exploded. Why did he waste money getting us the best, the most delicious food? Silently we sat, appetites gone. Mother cleared the plates away. Father flounced off and slammed the door.

Where did he go? What was he doing? Mother glanced after him. There were now five children, for two more girls had been born: Rita, whom everyone called Dolly because she was so pretty with big, dark eyes and dark brown curly hair rather like the Japanese-made dolls with "cute American faces", and Marcella two years younger who had lighter brown hair and eyes. I thought of them as "the children" because I was eight years older than Dolly and 10 when Marcella arrived.

Father was still handsome, still magnetic, still the patriarch with big ideas and I believe that mother, who was better educated than he, and fastidious and talented was still in love with him. But it had become a resentful relationship. She could not be noisy, party loving, exuberant as he was. However there were other women who could, and would.

We had a telephone in our house. It was the old upright kind with the receiver hanging on the side and sometimes neighbours used to ask if they could use it. Some women used it as an excuse to call and see father, which upset my mother. "Leave him alone. He's married and he's got a family," she'd snap at them. She cried and felt miserable with the betrayal and shame.

One-day father came home with a broken nose delivered by another woman's husband. "Serves you right," mother said. "You asked for it. Those women are nothing but…"

"Well what sort of wife are you?" father shouted after her. "You won't do anything. You won't even entertain my friends…"

The rows were full of bitterness, recrimination, and they were becoming more frequent. Father stayed out more often. My mother's despair and unhappiness settled like a pall over our home.

# Chapter 6

One of the reasons for my mother's unhappiness was that she suspected father kept bad company. She did not need to be much of a detective to put that together: to start with there seemed to be a lot of money coming into our house and father was a big spender. And what she saw of his friends did not please her at all. His vagueness about the 'business' (this was the period of the Italian mobster gangs) made her very uneasy. Some women may have enjoyed the fur coats and asked no questions, but mother was not one of them.

My father had the raw energy of a new immigrant in a hurry to make his fortune and a young man's restless taste for adventure. He did not waste much time in the barber's shop but while he was there his talent for making friends drew into his life some clients who would be useful business contacts later.

Father's enthusiasm was infectious. He always had ideas. They were legal on the whole—I do not believe he was a dishonest man, at least not at this time—and if it comes to risk, where is the successful businessman who would not take a chance?

Father's strength was that he was a persuasive talker. He had little enough money to invest himself, but his plans appeared to be such obvious winners that his friends, who did have the money wondered why no one else had latched on.

Even before he was demobbed from the Army, he had a plan unfolding. There was a post-war appetite for fun in the air; young people wanted to dance, dress up, drink cocktails. He would import alcohol. Most hardheaded businessman would have looked at the growing temperance movement sweeping America as in Europe and Britain and concluded that the liquor-importing business was not the ideal one to get involved with at this time. Part of being a successful businessman is to have good timing. Father's timing was awful.

There had been a shortage of spirits during the war because it was considered unpatriotic to use grain to make alcohol, and a number of brewers and distillers had German names. So there was, if you ignored the temperance movement, a growing potential market. True, Kansas had been 'dry' since 1884 and many public figures and anti-alcohol organisations like the Women's Christian Temperance Union were vocal and constantly batting for prohibition but then they would. When John D. Rockefeller donated $35,000 to the Anti-Saloon League, he was the only big name to do so. But by 1919, three quarters of the US had approved an amendment banning the "sale or transportation of intoxicating liquors" and the next year, the whole country went under prohibition.

By this time father and his "business friends" must have been already involved in the liquor business. I was too young to know much about it and my mother kept to herself, but the only conclusion I can draw looking back is that my father became a bootlegger.

Although prohibition drew in the crooks and the mobsters, the idea of flouting a law which seemed killjoy and pointless while making a healthy profit, appealed to many of the adventurous young. Father probably enjoyed what seemed to be harmless risk-taking and he relished the profits.

Reading contemporary reports, the "transportation of intoxicating liquors" and consumption of them in riotous parties became almost a national sport. A visiting German wrote of how he sat on a cushion, noticed feeling increasingly damp, and realised he had caused a leak in his hostess's unconventional brandy container. He said that people filled the spare tyres of their cars with whisky, that a child's teddy bear or doll might conceal a flask... Some people were caught and did time and some rich people were caught and paid others to do their time for them.

"Bathtub gin" was being made in so many houses there could scarcely have been a party that was not lubricated by it, or where you could not buy homemade supplies. There was a family living across the street from us who were obviously up to something. They were very mysterious—well-dressed men going in and out and they had big cars parked outside. They were not really part of the neighbourhood—they were different. We gossiped about them. One night there was a lot of noise as if a fight was going on so the neighbours called the police.

The law came in a big Ford station wagon with a Black Maria behind. Policemen clamoured out, brandishing their clubs, smashed on the door and ordered everyone within to "come out into the street."

It was a warm summer evening with the moon coming up. The front door of our house was open to let a breeze blow through and we were sitting on the steps, when suddenly people started running out of the raided house like ants. There were lots of girls; flappers in short beaded dresses, high heels and bright red lipstick, their bobbed hair and necklaces flying.

A few of them dashed across the narrow cobbled road, straight up our steps, through the open door, pushed past my mother who was standing in the hall, out through the kitchen at the end, into the yard and scrambled over the five-foot fence. As they ran I could hear their rows of beads clacking against each other and the clatter of their high heels and I smelled a mingled whiff of perfume and alcohol.

The five of them got away, and no doubt came back to play another day. I can imagine it must have seemed fun—until it became serious. And one day it did.

My father who went out daily "on business" was arrested. The police came and took him away from the house. Mother was horrified and ashamed. Father protested his innocence.

The charge involved a raid on a government warehouse of confiscated liquor during which a security guard had been killed. Brutality was not my father's line and he was acquitted. Whether he was an accessory or not, he certainly did not look the part in the dock: more like a distinguished gentleman, immaculately but quietly dressed and well spoken. His considerable charm had full play and the local newspaper, the Evening Bulletin which reported the case at the time said he defended himself with such eloquence, the judge and jury concluded that far from driving the getaway car, he had had nothing to do with the crime. But he was mixing with the wrong people. And mother was not going to make his friends welcome under her roof.

Being only a child of about eight at the time, I adored father because he was kind and amusing when he was not in a rage, whereas mother spent a lot of time silent or complaining. As I was the eldest she confided more in me than anyone else: I think I must have been her only confidant because she spoke to nobody else, and at times I felt like the mother. I was expected to do a lot of housework, general cleaning up and tidying. "If you love me you will do this for me," was a line I heard often. Mother sewed, played the piano expertly, made the house look lovely. But she did not like cooking or entertaining.

Father of course loved entertaining and he wanted to invite his rather too smartly dressed friends home, as he often did. Mother always cleared off out of the way. He wanted to show off his good-looking wife and to impress them with fine food, perhaps a tune or two on the $1,000 Lester piano. His friends were noisy. They liked a good laugh, their gold jewellery glowed in the gaslight, and they were all great pals. Some of them even had a touch of class. Mother did not like them. Nor did she like cooking. (Her version of Italian cuisine was to add a handful of raisins. She put them in everything, including meatballs.) She would leave father to his cronies and retire to her room to read or sew.

One day father invited some of his business friends home to lunch and he was determined to put up a good show, impress them with his social standing, his status as husband of a beautiful and talented wife and children.

He warned mother that he expected her to play hostess. She was to entertain them and not retreat to her bedroom. They would want refreshments. She must cook.

"No," said mother. "I do not like your friends. You can entertain them yourself." She turned to leave. Father was furious and grabbed her by the shoulders and shook her, shouting, "You'll do as I say."

Angrily she went to the kitchen. She rattled the cutlery, took a few things down from the shelves, started half-heartedly to make some sweet rice cakes. Father's friends started to arrive. They came in expensive cars and greeted each other loudly with much backslapping.

"Theresa, come out and meet our guests," called father, and mother emerged stony-faced from the kitchen to be introduced. Father covered over as best he could, making jokes, pouring generous tots of illegal gin, trying to draw her into the conversation. Mother's expression did not shift. She looked contemptuously from face to face, stood up even straighter than usual, raised her chin and stalked out, up to her room, where she stayed.

Her worst fears had been confirmed and she was shocked. These were not the sort of people she should be asked to meet. They were crooks. Flashy. Vulgar criminals.

Father was amazed. So were his guests. Then he started talking a little faster than usual. He said Theresa had been unwell lately, she still felt weak. Never mind, drink up. He went into the kitchen to make the refreshments himself, a few sandwiches, nuts, and how about a good plate of spaghetti? Father was a good cook and usually an enthusiastic one. He could improvise with sauces, tossing in the fresh herbs—basil and oregano from the garden, pasta with mussels, everything con brio, leaving the kitchen in a mess. But this time he was furious and cursing under his breath. The guests wandered in and made some good-natured comments, pretending nothing had happened.

When they had gone we children heard my father shouting. I had never seen him quite so angry. We cringed with fear and kept out of his way when he stormed upstairs and roared at mother. She was undaunted and icy. Her voice carried down the stairs. "Those men are gangsters," she said. "I never want to see them again."

"You put on airs," father shouted, "you think you're so grand and better than anyone else. Where do you imagine this house comes from, your piano, your fine clothes? What buys them? Well I'll tell you: it's my work, my business, my friends. That's what's buying you your fancy life, and don't forget it."

He crashed out of the house slamming the front door. I saw him get into his red touring car, jerk it into gear and go. We did not see him again for a week. We had been through it all before, but every time it seemed to get worse, a step towards a bigger disaster.

# Chapter 7

In 1925, when I was eleven years old, we left Hicks Street and went to live in Drexel Park, a green suburb west of the city. Despite all, father was going up in the world and we went with him.

I watched with a mixture of excitement and dismay as the furniture was loaded into a removal van, men staggered under the weight of the piano, the heavy sideboard from the dining room, dozens of boxes containing mother's hats, and all our toys... Then I wandered from empty room to room, saying goodbye to our old home. Already it seemed to echo and belong to someone else.

The neighbours who observed the loading-up with curiosity came out on their doorsteps to wave us off. Then carrying our most precious things, our favourite dolls and mother's best dress, we four children crammed into the back of father's shining red car, father and mother settled regally in front with baby Marcella who was just one year old on mother's lap, and off we sped to a new and more splendid life.

Leonard and I twisted round to wave to our friends. Marie, a year and a half younger than me was quiet and liked to play by herself and Dolly was only three years old, so they did not have street playmates, but Leonard and I did.

On countless warm summer evenings the girls had put chalk marks on the paving stones to play hopscotch, or tied a rope between lamp posts to skip and jump over it, and showed off their dolls, while the boys kicked their balls down the street and climbed the poles to swing on the crossbars of the gas lamps.

Now we waved goodbye to them all and shouted that we would call back, but we never did.

Mother was glad to be leaving. We were going to a smarter place. And when we saw our new home, we were pleased and excited, too.

It was a much bigger and lighter house than the one we had left in Hicks Street. This was in Fairfax Road. And Fairfax Road was the latest source of father's wealth, for he and his friend Alessio had built five of the houses there.

After the war, one of father's moneymaking ideas had been to get into the property business. Of course he had no money but his friend Alessio did. So with father pulling the strings and using his contacts they acquired some half-built houses in the green belt on the west side of the Schuylkill River just beyond the burgeoning city, and finished them as the sort of homes for better-off people who liked to live in sylvan surroundings while enjoying the facilities of a city.

Now we were joining them. My mother saw these people as a more suitable type of neighbour for one with her position in society. It was not a view that lasted, but at least we all liked the house, especially father, because he had designed it himself.

Lack of self-confidence was never father's problem. He may have been just a barber and a part-time bootlegger, but when he had one of his ideas he was brilliant at enthusing his rich friends. His idea on this occasion had been to copy Spanish-style houses, like some he had seen when he once visited California.

He had talked about those wonderful villas, each one semi-detached, with French doors at the back leading to a garden, and little wrought- iron balconies. "We could create a village by

Drexel Hill. We'll call it Drexel Park: we could make a fortune."
Alessio agreed absolutely. Poor Alessio: when the crash came
and all his money had all gone, he killed himself. And my father
went on to further adventures. But that was later.

For now, we busied ourselves exploring and admiring our
new home. Alessio called round for a drink. Yes, he agreed,
Michael had got it right. Houses were just what were needed after
the war, and this little corner of urban countryside was the perfect
site and Spanish villas were the perfect style.

I dashed from room to room shouting with delight,
Leonard and Marie at my heels while mother tried to calm us at
the same time as supervising the removal men staggering under
the weight of her precious piano.

The parlour was the biggest room. It had a large fireplace,
and casement windows that opened out instead of ordinary sash
windows, and a French door leading to a big garden. A stuccoed
garage at the bottom awaited the red car. There were several trees
and one very tall pine in the garden and like the icing on the cake,
an owl that sat in it and hooted mournfully at night like a visitor
from a romantic book.

The dining room also had a fireplace: it was a big family
room where we had all our meals and did our homework. The
kitchen was small, but as mother admitted, perfectly equipped,
and upstairs there was a bathroom and three bedrooms.

For a family with five children that may not sound
extravagant, but it was a big advance on our cramped little house
in Hicks Street. And now, thought father, he had a fine villa in
which to entertain and impress his influential friends.

The furniture was unloaded but it was not enough. Father
bought more: carpets, beautiful tables and chairs, bolts of heavy
silk and damask for mother to sew into curtains.

Out on the lawn we could see squirrels and birds—a blue
jay and pigeons fluttered in the trees, and maybe there would be
hedgehogs at night. Mother was pleased. She thought that now, at
last, we had got away from the obnoxious female neighbours who
had pushed their way into our house in Hicks Street on the

pretext of borrowing the telephone and flirted insolently with her husband. Could it be a new start?

I was like my mother's agony aunt. "Yes", I said. And I knew I should have said "No".

A leopard does not change its spots by moving to different territory and father certainly had no intention of changing his. He liked women. In the plural.

Because I was so often my mother's confidante I started to side with her. It wasn't fair: she was a good mother, the house was clean and pretty and she was affectionate to the children, at any rate, when we were small.

Father though, was much livelier company. Mother played the piano, but it was he who used to take Leonard, Marie and me, all dressed up, to the opera where we would sit in a box overlooking the glittering company and nod off to sleep. As he picked me up my head rested on his shoulder and he smelled reassuringly of good tobacco and shaving cream and cologne… I remember jerking awake as the singer hit a high note.Father hissed in my ear, "How could you go to sleep when the great Caruso is singing!"

He loved opera. And he might shout when he was in a rage but he never raised a hand against us. Sometimes he put on the angry roar just to make us laugh.

My own musical tastes were not at all highbrow. Mother had taught me how to play some simple tunes on the piano but I preferred to make up my own, especially when my father was sitting in his armchair reading the newspaper. I liked the part where he would throw his paper on the floor, jump up and shout, " Stop! Enough!"

One day I was playing my favourite made-up piece, Storm in the Meadow which started quietly and rose to tremendous thumps and crashes and as I banged my way through the storm I kept glancing over to him waiting for the shout of anger and newspaper flung to the floor. But he was taking no notice. He was engrossed in something. Eventually I got off the stool and went over to see what he was doing.

"These are soldiers," he said, showing me little figures he had been drawing around the margin of his newspaper. Would you like me to show you how to draw them?"

"Yes," I said, immediately interested. I forgot the piano. I was captivated. I drew soldiers, and cats, and the bird in the garden, and father and mother and the house... It was the start of a lifelong compulsion, a career, an addiction that has nourished me and raised my spirits though all my life's journey. After that I was never without a pencil and my drawing pad. Father must have been amazed that his ruse had worked so well.

Meanwhile all of us children and mother revelled in our new house in the country. It was summer; we could play on the cool grass in the garden, hear the wind in the trees and the creek of the swing next door when the old lady who lived there sat on it and rocked gently while she read her books. At night, the owl visited my dreams. And for the first time I understood the changing of seasons, noticed the first flowers in spring and the leaves falling in autumn.

The grass grew high and neglected in our garden, which was separated from the one next door by a wire fence. The neighbour's Great Dane was tied to the wire. I wanted to cut our grass but it was too long to mow so our neighbour lent me a scythe and I worked all day till I had blisters on my hand. It was slow work: at this rate it would take a week to finish—but I have always been practical and I had an idea for speeding things up. I dug a trench around the lawn, stood by for emergencies with the water hose, and set the lawn, which was tinder-dry alight. It burned very well. A little too well for the neighbours, who were upset and called the fire brigade. But I had the trench as a fire-brake and hosepipe at the ready so it did no damage. When the grass grew again it was a nice lawn, just like the neighbour's and I was able to keep it short with a push mower they lent me. Later I planted vegetables, and it was thrilling to watch onions and carrots coming up. The peas did not work. I pulled them up to see how they were doing and they died.

Our new school, for boys and girls, was a short bus ride through broad tree-lined streets to a road by the park. It was called Garreforge School and the head mistress; Miss Kirk had a reputation for being very progressive, insisting on every child learning another language (I did Spanish because they said it was 'commercial') and on every teacher being properly qualified. It was one of the best schools I ever went to. There was even an art teacher, and my happiness overflowed. Life was golden and everything was going to be all right after all.

Except that life does not run on straight tracks. It veers and turns unexpectedly and suddenly the view changes, as soon it did.

They seemed to argue every day: mother defiant, father loud and furious, and it usually ended the same way: father stomping angrily out of the house and slamming the door behind him.

His absences became more frequent and lasted longer. Mother told me he had "another interest." Soon he was spending less time with us than with the other interest. And soon we were finding that being Italian in Drexel Park was not at all like being part of a warm, noisy, Italian home-from-home in Hicks Street.

Most of the people here were German Lutherans and they did not like Catholics. There were a few Irish, and we at the time were the only Italians. Italians, we soon learned, were at the very bottom of the heap.

At school, with a name like Emmanuella Circelli, there was no mistaking where my family came from. "Spaghetti benders! Wops! Dagos!" other children shouted. "Wo-ops! Go back home!" Playtime and travelling were the danger times, away from the protection of the teachers and sometimes the bullies ganged up to beat us up.

Every day as soon as lessons ended I dashed off to get Leonard and my sisters Dolly and Maria and we huddled in the school bus together ignoring the taunts. Sometimes we were in tears by the time we reached home. Once, from fear of a big, beefy boy who had hit me, I stayed away from school for a week.

What could we do? I did not want to upset mother and father was hardly ever at home any more. One day on the way to school, the bus was so packed I had to stand and found myself pushed up beside the beefy bully. He turned and saw me—and with a leer grabbed both my wrists. "Da-go, Spaghetti-bender," he started chanting and as he did so he twisted my right wrist. His face was close to mine. I glared at him and gritted my teeth against the pain. I felt tears in my eyes—the sight of which seemed to pleasantly distract him, for he relaxed his grip.

I jerked my right hand free, and slammed my fist into his mouth. My knuckles broke his two front teeth and he put both his hands over his face and yelled and spat out blood and to my joy started to cry.

There was silence in the bus. I held my head up. Whatever happened next, I would be glad I'd hit him. No one was taunting us now.

As soon as we reached the school, the boy ran in with his hand over his mouth and into the head master's office. His parents were notified. Both his father and mother came to school to fetch him and warned the principal that they would be seeking compensation from that Italian girl's parents; their son would need expensive dental work... those Italians could pay.

The principal called me to his office and I showed him my swollen wrist. "He's been bullying me for weeks," I said. "He's been hitting me and calling me names ..."

"They say you'll have to pay for his teeth."

"I can't," I said. I couldn't tell my mother, she had troubles of her own.

"I'll look into it," said the head. A few days later he called me and said, "I don't think you will have any more trouble. And by the way, I don't blame you for what you did."

He was right about the trouble: that was the end of it. The message went around: "leave them alone because the tall girl fights back."

# Chapter 8

Once the school bully had been encouraged to leave us alone, I started to enjoy going to school and made friends. "We're going to Indian Basin on Saturday," one of them said to me as the week drew to its close. "You coming?"

I thought of mother. Father would probably be with his other interest and mother would complain if I was not around to do things in the house. "If you love me you'll …" I could hear her refrain.

"Yes," I said. "But I don't know where it is."

"Come with us." We walked across the railway track, down roads and over fields until we reached the woods, a magical place with a stream where we could paddle, and caves that Red Indians had used when the land was theirs, and where you could still find arrowheads lying on the ground. We played hide and seek, and collected some chipped stone arrowheads, then slowly trailed the mile or so home.

The discovery of Indian Basin enhanced my life at Drexel Park and I returned often, usually on my own with a book and a drawing pad.

One day I took Marie with me. She was a sickly child with chronic kidney trouble and spent a lot of time on her own, while the two youngest, Dolly and Marcella played with each other. Marie was pleased to come with me but as we crossed the railway track, the metal lines changed and her foot was jammed between two rails. I tugged and she pulled, both terrified and keeping an eye on the horizon. In the distance we saw an on-coming train. It was like one of those films where the heroine is tied to the tracks by the villain but there was no wild-eyed hero galloping to the rescue, so I gave a terrific yank that freed her and we both ran, leaving her shoes behind.

After that we paddled in the stream and explored the woods, but Marie's ankle hurt so we went home. There was hardly any traffic on the roads. The milkman and coal merchant and most of the other tradesmen used horses and carts so when we wandered off, sometimes for hours at a time, mother was never frightened of us coming to harm. We told her about Marie losing her shoes and Maria said she had had enough of Indian Basin and would not go again. Mother was concerned but not angry. She was not a shouter. But the stress of living with a husband who was absent most of the time was starting to change her.

She was becoming permanently anxious. Father called home and gave us money when he remembered, but he did not remember often enough. When he did come mother accused him of keeping other women, getting them to spy on her and said the neighbours were peering at her through the windows and plotting to entice him away. She wanted to move. Father refused. He said it would be just the same wherever we went. Mother spent a lot of time crying.

This made her seem paranoid, but she had a point. Strange women used to call at our house looking for father. On one occasion an expensive-looking one smothered in furs and jewellery rolled up to our front door in her chauffeur-driven limo, alighted and confronted mother with a "reasonable proposition." "You see, my dear, Michael and I are so in love," she gushed, "so you must let him go. I'm ready to offer you a substantial sum. You must understand, I'm the one he truly loves."

Mother slammed the door. Father had managed to convince yet another rich woman that she was the light of his life. And she was too naive, or too rich, to work out that he had lots of true loves.

We were not sure which one he was currently staying with, and when mother asked his parents they said they did not know either. Mother had always kept clear of his family, but my grandmother was a gentle, dignified woman, concerned for us all and she was very upset seeing us neglected. My grandfather who had worked hard as a tailor and bought my father the barber's shop was so angry he refused to speak to his son.

Up to this point father had been making enough money to keep us in reasonable comfort although he was very unreliable. He now rarely called at home. I used to go to the barber's shop to meet him, or sometimes for lunch at a restaurant when he would hand over enough money to keep us going for a week or so.

I hated going to the shop. It was here that father met some of the moneyed and influential men he used to further his many schemes. When I called to persuade him to give us money to buy food for the week, he would keep me waiting like a punishment for being there. "But Daddy, what are we doing to do?" I'd plead after sitting there for hours reading a book. His reply was impatient and dismissive. "I can't help it. I haven't got any more."

His salon near the station in west Philadelphia was quite smart and had several staff including a manicurist who was a plain little woman with pale blue eyes. I knew he had been sleeping with her.

One day I saw she had been crying. Her eyes were pink and her face flushed and when she saw me, she started crying again and beckoned me to her room. "I gave your father all my savings," she said. "He said he would pay it back, but now he says he can't, and I've got nothing to live on. You must tell your father that I've got nothing. I don't know what to do."

What could I do but say that I was sorry? I knew she would never get her savings back. She wasn't the first and would not be the last. He even "sold" a house that didn't exist to my mother's mother, relieving her of her savings—and she didn't even like him.

In that tight community around the Italian market, gossip spread fast and father had a name for philandering and leaving women in the lurch. I heard there was an Italian woman, one of his lovers, who had given birth to a son who looked like me. I never saw her. And now to the poor plain little manicurist who must have loved and trusted him enough to forget he was some other woman's husband, all I could say was "Sorry". She looked at me with her big washed-out blue eyes, and said sadly, "And I am sorry for you, too."

Well might she have been, for father now had another scheme in mind, which involved a business deal in Ohio. And to pull it off he needed to look like an upright and responsible family man. The dependable family man was the self-image he liked best, even when other women were calling at the house for him, to my mother's distress. Even coming back drunk and sometimes hitting her—though he never touched his children— did not dent this conceit. I used to shout, "Don't, Daddy," and climbed on to the table so that I could reach him and bit him to make him stop. "You little devil" he once shouted at me when I hit him with a book.

Acting the family man was more difficult now that he had dumped the family, so he decided to take steps to have the children back by applying for custody of them in court.

I went to court with my mother and was allowed to stand beside her. She sat crying while my father explained to the judge that she was not a fit mother; that mentally she was unable to cope and he was afraid for our well-being.

I was distraught with fear that he would persuade everyone he was a gentleman and honest, which was what he was good at. I put my hand on mother's arm and wouldn't look at him. But the judge seemed not to be impressed because he beckoned to me and said, "Come up here. I want to speak to you. Now you tell me in your own words—and there's no hurry—just tell me how your mother cares for you. Does she get food for you?"

"Yes", I said.

"Does she take care of you?"

"Yes. And she makes our clothes. She made this dress."

"Your father says she sees other men. Is this true?"

"No, sir!" I said. "She never sees anybody, except for us. She's kind to us. She cleans the house—it's the cleanest house I've ever been in and she does everything. She's a good mother, ask my brother and sisters if you like, she's a very good mother, honestly she is."

Father was refused custody. He was absolutely furious and as I went past him, he said through his teeth, "You'll regret this for the rest of your life."

The split from my mother was now permanent. After that I used to meet father at irregular intervals in a restaurant for lunch and he would hand over some housekeeping money for me to give her.

We had our last meeting on Tuesday, the 29th of October 1929. I remember the date exactly because it was one that would figure in the history of America and of the world and mark the start of our descent into poverty. But then to me it seemed like any other day: mild, autumnal, a few leaves starting to drop from the trees—and I sat at one of the round tables waiting.

As I wondered what had happened to father, I grew hungrier and started looking at the menu. Then I saw him coming, dodging across the road, into the restaurant, but not the immaculate, self-confident father I knew. He was dishevelled, his coat flew open and his eyes were bleary red. He flung himself down on a chair, and tried to speak, but he was incoherent.

"I'm hungry, Daddy," I started. "Could I have soup today as well as …"

"How can you talk about eating when the whole world is collapsing?" he shouted. He looked so wild, his movements were jerky and he got up and sat down again. "I haven't got any money, don't you understand? Nobody's got any money. Everything has crashed. Haven't you seen the headlines in the newspapers?"

Of course I had not. Otherwise I would have read that the financial world had crashed, that billions of dollars had been lost and this day, known ever after as "Black Tuesday" was a day of panic and ruin across the states as investors jostled to sell 16 million shares.

Like wildfire the panic spread across the world. Now I could see that father's desperation was mirrored in the faces of hurrying figures outside in the street.

The waitress came to our table with her notebook, pencil poised for the orders. Father pushed back his chair. "Here," he said throwing some coins on the table, "that's for your lunch. And this"—he threw a $20 bill on the table—"is for your mother. Tell her that's all she's getting. I'm broke." He got up and hurried out. And that was the last any of us saw of him for more than a year.

We heard that his business partner Alessio who had put up the money for the Drexel Park scheme committed suicide. Father was of tougher material, but creditors were after him. Insecurity was descending and he deserted us.

# Chapter 9

I hurried home to tell mother. At 15 years old and mature for my age from looking after the smaller children, I took coping with problems in my stride, but mother was simply not equipped for dealing with want and neglect.

Her own mother was strong and practical, one of the first to take an active interest in women's rights and education in Philadelphia—but Theresa had been her youngest child, the most beautiful one, spoilt and educated in the gentler feminine arts of needlework, music and literature. She had the upbringing of a lady who did not expect to earn her own living. As far as mother was concerned, she was a wife, and it was a husband's job to keep his wife. It was obvious that her husband had no intention of doing so but she clung stubbornly to the idea. And did she, in spite of all her hurt pride and anger, love him still? I think the answer must have been "yes", for unknown to us when father left for the last time, she was pregnant once again.

The miscarriage came as a shock. Mother screamed for help from her bedroom. I dashed upstairs and saw her lying on sheets covered in blood, eyes wide as she cried, "Help, I'm bleeding to death!" I ran terrified to a neighbour who came in and called the doctor and he arranged at once for mother to go to hospital where she stayed for three weeks.

While she was away all five of us children were so frightened, we slept together in one bed for comfort and prayed every night for mother. Neighbours came in each day to give us food. When mother came back from hospital, her own mother and sister Rose came by train with baskets of food for us all, only to be greeted with the by-now familiar petulance. "I don't want your charity. I'm not a beggar. I've got a husband and it's his job to look after me."

Some hope. In the beginning we managed on our own.

Mother would not appeal to her own parents because that would be like admitting she made a mistake in running away to get married, so she relied on her children, Leonard and me.

Leonard was only 10 but he was tall, strong and optimistic. He felt protective towards her, and his cheerfulness—he was always whistling and telling her not to worry—kept up our morale.

"We could sell a few things, Mom," he suggested. "I don't want toys now. Let's sell them." Mother had never liked the over-expensive toys father used to buy for us so she agreed without much of a struggle. And she had a fine collection of crystal and silver she could sell. She had never been friendly with the neighbours but they must have known we had problems because they bought things from her. The first things she sold were her fur coats. She also had some building bonds, acquired when father was making money and she took those to the bank and sold them. The money lasted us several weeks.

For the moment things were not too bad and we all carried on going to school. I started to do well at athletics and art, and at home I often slipped into the garden next door where Miss McNichol, a retired schoolmistress used to sit on the swing under the tree on summer evenings reading and knitting.

Miss McNichol was Irish and she lived with another retired schoolmistress called Betty. Her sister, Anne McNichol who was very small and thin, kept house for them.

They were artistic, educated women. Their garden was an oasis, their friendship a source of comfort and they had a big library, which they shared with us. I loved reading books. It was my passion, especially travel books and often I went to Indian Basin with my favourites, borrowed copies of Aesop's Fables, The Count of Monte Cristo and Robinson Crusoe.

On warm evenings I sat on the swing with Miss McNichol—there were two seats hanging from a frame facing each other under an awning—and she told me about her travels, wonderful stories about the art and antiquities of Italy and the rest of Europe. I was entranced. As we moved, the swing squeaked and Miss McNichol carried on with her knitting, glancing up from time to time to smile at me. She said she was going to retire to Sorrento one day. She had been there by boat and it had taken two weeks from Philadelphia.

I picked up a book called The Well of Loneliness from a table in her library and looked at it curiously. I'd heard of it. She snatched it from me: "You won't want to read that," she said and put it in her study. I think it was by a lesbian but I did not understand what that meant. I only knew that Miss McNichol was a refined lady who treated me always with understanding and kindness.

I used to tell her everything, about the problems at home, and how we had been bullied at school because we were Italian. She was indignant and told me always to be proud of my roots because Greece and Italy were the birthplaces of western culture. She realised we were hard up so she asked my mother if she could rent the garage at the bottom of our garden for $5 a week. That helped us a lot. One day my mother asked her if she would knit me a suit instead of paying the rent because I had grown out of all my clothes and she made me a beautiful blue suit which I wore all the time.

When we ran out of money again mother sold her collection of silver and crystal goblets. Neighbours bought them. Mother would never have accepted help for nothing because she was too proud but selling was different. She did not have to feel beholden. The wind-up gramophone with the "His Master's Voice" dog on the trumpet went after the silver, and all the records—except for my father's precious Carusos which mother had smashed in a rage.

The piano stayed. Mother's family again helped by buying things—the only way mother would accept money from them. And in the end, when we were forced from the house, grandmother bought the precious piano and took it back to her own small house where she already had her own, and managed to squeeze it in to the sitting room with the other one.

Because of all the worry and stress it was not long before mother became ill again and the doctor said she had a stomach ulcer and should go into hospital. This time she refused. What would the family do without her? I stayed away from school to help. Winter was coming. We had no money to buy coal or to pay the gas bills. It was freezing cold. Even the water was turned off and I had to go and fetch it in a bucket from the fountain down the road.

Every day mother bought a bag of rice and some milk— just that, day after day, and nothing else and that was what we lived on. The vegetables I grew in the garden, onions, potatoes and carrots had all gone. Mother sold the furniture and had the gas turned back on so that she could cook but we were still freezing and had too little to cook.

When we went down to the shops we could see others faring even worse than ourselves. Poverty was visible everywhere and there an air of desperation. Well-dressed men sold matches and shoelaces at street corners, and apples from little baskets, polishing the fruit then tucking their hands under their arms against the cold. They were haggard and diminished and you could feel the fear. They had mortgaged their homes and lost the money. Some were just begging. Queues stood outside the soup kitchen, pitiful sights I had never witnessed before, and in the newspapers there were reports every day of bankrupted businessmen committing suicide just as Alessio had. Billboards throughout the city carried notices of houses being sold off by the sheriff after bank foreclosures.

All this time Leonard was cheerful and kept telling mother, "Don't worry. I'll take care of you." He could even make her laugh. But there was less and less to laugh about and we were desperate. It was so cold and damp in the house that the wallpaper mother had so carefully chosen now flopped down off the walls, and perhaps worst of all, we were hungry all the time.

Leonard found himself a job delivering newspapers early in the mornings before going to school and I had a part-time job in a candy shop. It was all I could get. This was a time when 15 million men were unemployed.

Our small earnings were not enough to feed the family. I passed the queue outside the soup kitchen every day and was daily tempted to join it, but the line stretched round the block and there was a separate one to get the bread. It took about two hours. And besides, you couldn't take anything back for the family, and I would have felt guilty eating myself. Mother of course would have forbidden any of us to "accept charity". Once I spent five cents on a cup of coffee at a little place with porcelain tables where people stood eating lunch and girls served drinks from two urns, one with boiling water. People would come in with mugs and ask just for the boiling water, and take tomato ketchup from a table to put in the water so that it tasted like hot soup, and that was all they would have for the day. I never saw those girls turn anyone away.

The knowledge of others being worse off than ourselves was no consolation. If anything it added to our fear. But Leonard was ever optimistic. "Never mind, I can find a better job," he said, and went off whistling down to a chain store and asked if they would give him some work delivering groceries at the weekends.

"How old are you, boy?" the manager asked. Leonard was tall, but he was only 10. "We need the money, sir" he explained.

"Yes, yes" the manager said. He knew our family. He knew we were destitute. "All right. So you are 15, eh? Start tomorrow morning."

Leonard was there early. They gave him a wooden cart full of the orders and a list of addresses, and he pushed the heavy load along the roads. By night time when the store was shutting, he was tired and exhausted, but he had his pay and in addition the kindly manager handed him a bag of damaged vegetables.

So he came home as he had left, whistling cheerfully and handed the bag to mother. "Now you can make some soup," he said with a big grin. "I had those for nothing. They were left over. Nothing wrong with them really, look..."

Mother was horrified. She snatched the bag and threw it across the room. "People have no right to send us garbage," she shouted. "We're not beggars!"

Leonard started to cry. Mother stormed out to her room. "Don't cry," I said to Leonard. "I'll pick them up and clean them and we'll have the soup. We'll all have plenty. I'm going to Betty's father to ask him for some bones to boil as well." Betty was my school friend and her father was a butcher. They lived over their shop, so when I asked for bones to make soup he fetched me two big ones with pieces of meat still on it. I boiled it with Leonard's onions and potatoes and carrots and a few shreds of cabbage and the delicious smell wafted through the house. Mother said she would not touch it.

We laid the table for the feast, all hungry for the treat. Mother stayed in her room. But later she crept down and ate her share.

Leftover vegetables boiled with soup bones became our regular fare, supplemented with bread and milk bought with the meagre sums Leonard and I managed to earn. Poverty had driven down prices so milk was 10 cents a quart and we could buy a loaf of bread for a nickel. But we were so hungry, I thought of food all the time, and it must have been worse for Leonard, who was growing fast.

There were days when there were extras, like the half-dozen cracked eggs the manager gave to Leonard at the end of one week. "Don't show them to mother," I told him. "Just give them to me and I'll make a big omelette for us all."

That's what I did. Mother had some too, pretending not to know where they had come from. Sometimes I almost hated her, the way she was so concerned for herself, her silly pride while we all starved. "We are not beggars … I've got a husband who should be keeping me"—I was sick of hearing it. But Leonard was still devoted to her, still assuring her that we would all be fine. We bought some hot water bottles so that we could be warm enough to sleep at night.

As Christmas approached and she became busier, the owner of the candy shop gave me more work and sometimes I had a bag of broken sweets to take home. We divided them out on Christmas day.

All through the winter months I had not been able to go to school and now February came and it was snowing heavily. It was Saturday and I made the usual pot of soup out of boiled bones and vegetables. Leonard was delivering the last of the orders in his wooden cart, and because he was still only eleven years old and the snow was coming down in a blizzard I told mother that I would go and wait for him outside the shop so that we could come home together.

I was sitting on a bench in the snow waiting, when a woman came up to me and said, "Your brother has been injured in an accident. He's been taken to hospital. I told the police that I know your mother, so I'll go home with you and I can drive you to the hospital."

We hurried home. I heard her telling mother, "It's very bad. It was a car."

"Let's drive up straight away, mother," I said. "Hurry: I'm ready."

Mother's expression had hardly changed. There were no tears, no questions. "No, we'll walk," she said.

The snow was deep on the ground and the hospital was a few miles away. "But mother…" I said.

"We can manage, thank you," I heard her say to the woman.

"But he is very badly hurt…" the woman thought mother had not taken it in, and maybe she hadn't because her face was set in an almost vacant expression. She showed the woman to the door.

I knew that mother did not want anyone to see that she was penniless and needed help. So we walked through the snow, sometimes struggling through drifts up to our knees in the dark, skidding and freezing and soaking wet. It took over an hour.

When we reached the hospital we went right in and were shown straight to the ward. The doctor standing by the bedside looked up, came over to speak and his first words were, "I'm sorry."

We learned what had happened. Leonard pushing his cart along the road and hardly visible in the snowstorm had been crushed by two cars skidding into each other. A number of bones were broken, one had pierced his lung and he had other severe internal injuries.

Now on the hospital bed he lay unconscious, a pale, greenish colour, breathing with difficulty. He half opened his eyes and murmured, "Mom, mom." Mother made no move. She did not cry. She held her hand over her mouth and just watched him. She said nothing. And I stood there too, watching without comprehension. "No, he can't be dying," I thought.

The police asked about father and sent a car to fetch him. Mother and I were still standing there looking at Leonard when father came in, face contorted and sobbing. "My son," he cried, "Oh, my dear son." Leonard was dying. He could not speak. But he saw father and turned his head away. Mother was still standing dry-eyed, watching with her hand over her mouth as if stifling a silent scream.

"I'd like you to move back," the doctor said softly as the crisis approached. Father stepped away. At that moment, my brother sat up in bed and held out his arms. He uttered just one sound, a drawn-out "Aaah", and his colour changed from the deathly green to its normal colour. He looked radiant as if full of light and he smiled. The nurse got down on her knees and Leonard fell back onto the bed. Mother bent over him. And to our horror, blood suddenly spurted from his eyes, his nose and his mouth, which was still smiling till it covered him and splashed on to us, and mother just stood there looking at him without expression, without crying, without saying a word, splashed with blood.

The doctor drew me to one side. "I would have felt much happier if your mother had shown some emotion," he murmured. "It is very bad, very serious that she does not even cry."

Father came over, still sobbing but I would not even look at him. If he had not abandoned us, Leonard would still be alive. I took mother's arm and we walked out of the hospital together.

When we got home, she went up to her room without speaking to anybody. She shed no tears. She did nothing. I put my younger sisters to bed and from then on took on mother's role.

My father, I heard later, sued the chain store for hiring a minor and won some money in court. He spent it all himself.

# Chapter 10

E ven now after a long and happy life filled with love, companionship and laughter the memory of Leonard's death brings back the surreal misery of that time. His dying was not the end. There was an autopsy, and then he had to be formally identified before burial.

I had a cousin called Sydney who was a doctor who came to help. Mother's stalwart Aunt Rose who had helped her to get married now came to run the house and Sydney took me to the coroner to do the identification. I was still a child myself, just 16, but my mother was in no state to go. Nor, for that matter was I, but more and more I had to assume the role of the adult and head of the family.

Like a nightmare, I remember the coroner who was about 6 ft 4 tall, gaunt and cadaverous. I thought, "There's something wrong with his face." Was it a tick? An expression? I could not concentrate. Sydney took me by my arm and I stumbled after an attendant who opened a door to a room with a bare electric bulb, a sharp, bright light in a house that seemed full of rubbish, old newspapers on the floors. We walked through into a tin shed at the back, where there were several bodies laid out, among them

Leonard covered in a sheet. After a lifetime the details are still hideously clear in my memory.

The attendant flicked off the cover with a swift movement and instead of just seeing the face, I found myself staring at Leonard's chest which had been cut open and roughly sewn together with string like a piece of meat. I trembled with shock, my teeth chattered and to my horror, I started to giggle. I was not amused. I could not stop giggling.

Sydney was angry with the attendant. "You could have just shown us the face," he said, and he took my arm again and put the pen in my shaking hand so that I could sign the identification papers. We left and Sydney stopped at the undertaker's and told him to get the body and hold it for burial. But the undertaker misunderstood. He took the body back to our house—it was common enough practice in those days—and laid Leonard out on one of the beds in the ice-cold bedroom. I was still weak and in shock, my teeth chattering, and I walked up and down stairs, calling in to see Leonard and talking to him, and laughing and giggling. "He moved, mummy. He moved!" I called out. My mother was upset. Aunt Rose led me gently downstairs and I started to cry and could not stop.

Leonard was buried a few days later. Grandmother was there, and mother's sister and we all wept and after that mother went over the frontier from sanity to wild and irrational behaviour from which she never returned.

Sometimes she was quiet and peaceful and I thought she was getting better, and then suddenly she would become violent and abusive. Once she attacked me with a pair of scissors and I fought for my life and escaped from the house. Her change of mood could be instant. Miss McNichol tried to tell me that mother could not help her behaviour, that it had nothing to do with me but was caused by all the worries she had.

Sometimes after a meal we would all gather round the piano and she played for us. She played the classics drawing out the beauty of the music, and sang, and we joined in with songs like Alice Blue Gown, Easter Bonnet, Au Claire de la Lune and carols. At Easter she made an effort to be cheerful and made little things from coloured paper for the youngest ones, Marcella who was now nearly six years old, and Dolly, two years older. Marie, aged 14, was still sickly and quiet. On these occasions mother was charming, pretty and like a young girl again as she told us stories about the family and her father who played the violin in a big orchestra. The sun seemed to shine once more bringing a warm sense of security and peace. Then suddenly, for no reason she would jump at me, uncontrollable, eyes bulging, physically changed as she shouted and struck out.

There was nothing I could do. There seemed no logical reason. Once it was because I had dropped the soap in the basin while I was washing. As time passed the good patches became fewer and the bad ones more frequent. Her paranoia about the neighbours increased. My two sources of solace were Miss McNichol's calm and gentle advice, and my retreat in Indian Basin where I could explore the woods and sit with my books.

As summer drew near we suffered less from the cold, but often we were without money for food or the gas to cook it with, even water, which was expensive in Philadelphia. Once father called with $20 and we had the gas and water turned back on but that did not last. I turned over in my mind ideas for earning more.

The grass was growing and I decided to hire myself as a lawn-cutter and gardener. I went around knocking at doors, my speech ready. "I know I'm not a boy but I am very strong and I'll mow your lawn for only 50 cents". I managed to cut four lawns, then dusty, hot and exhausted I went home with the two dollars.

Mother's mood, always on fragile switched to anger. "Is that all you made?" she shouted and hit my hand, scattering the coins on the floor. I bent to pick them up and she kicked them away. "Where's the rest of it? You've spent it yourself!" I managed to pick up three quarters, and then I ran from the house. I carried on running till I reached the railway station, and got on a train and went to the end of the line. It was dark when I got off and I did not know where I was. Fear and pain from a bleeding scratch on my arm made me sob as I sat on a tree stump by a long wall skirting a cemetery, terrified of staying there, and equally terrified of moving.

Unexpectedly from the darkness came the sound of a church bell. It was the sound of safety and I ran towards it, to the church, inside, to the priest who came out of his confessional box and I told him I had run away from my mother. I was crying so much, he took me to the sacristy, asked me if I was hungry, fetched a sandwich and glass of milk and gave me a dollar. Then he said, "Tell me about your mother." I said, "She has been very ill. She thinks everyone's against her. She thinks my father has given me money and I won't give it to her..." He said, "We'll have to do something about your mother," and he went to another room. Those words upset me. I thought people would come and take my mother away, so I got up and ran out, back to the train, back home, back to the fears I knew.

Somehow we struggled on and I even started going to school again. Occasionally father sent us money, then we could have the gas and water turned on again and buy enough food for a while before reverting to being hungry and cold. Most of the time mother was desperate. At the end of 69$^{th}$ street, about six blocks away was a fountain in the stone wall of a little park where people sat on benches round a patch of grass. The water in the fountain was pure and icy cold from a spring and it gushed from the mouth of a sculptured head. Several times a day I went there with a bucket and carried enough home for drinking, cooking and washing.

It was tiring and heavy work and I had a pain from a lump that appeared in my groin which the doctor—called by Miss McNichol—said was a hernia. "You must come to hospital and have a small operation," he said. "I can't," I said. "We have no money." He told us he would do it himself and it would cost nothing, but after lying in the hospital bed for a day and a half it went by itself and I went home.

The doctor's generosity and concern was typical of help given to us by a number of people at this time when so many families besides ours were hard up. It was unostentatious yet still had to run the gauntlet of mother's suspicions and pride. Children though can be more resilient than adults and in the midst of our problems, I still found life full of interest with discoveries to be made, new friends and endless things to learn.

About a mile from our house a shopping centre was being built. I had never seen anything like it before, it was so big, so grand. Two big stores fronted the entrance, not yet occupied, and as I walked by I saw that in one, a woman was sketching the portrait of another. I stopped to watch. It was fascinating so see how deftly her charcoal lines caught the shape of the face, the expression of the eyes, the posture from the slouch of the shoulders. The person doing the sketch was in her forties and no portrait herself: dumpy, in flat shoes, a loose top and shirt. But her drawing was brilliant. How she captured the expression... I watched until darkness started to fall and I had to go home.

I went again next day after school, and she was still there, still the same subject, the same picture which was almost finished. The sitter had left. The artist started putting away her charcoal and materials when she turned, saw me and beckoned me to her.

"So you are interested in drawing?" she asked.

"Yes, I've got a sketch book; I draw my friends and family.'

'Come here tomorrow', she said. 'I'd like to see them.'

Next day I went back. My sketches were in pencil because I did not have charcoal, but she said I had talent and that I caught the expression in my subjects' eyes. We became friends, and I went to see her often. She told me she had to earn her living and she was glad to have a place in the store where she could find customers because her cousin had been killed in the war leaving children whom she was trying to bring up as her own, and she could do it only because she had steady commissions for portraits. Some were very famous people, like the Duponts— naming a wealthy family in Delaware—and their children. Her son was now a famous conductor and musician and her own children had grown up.

I started visiting her often, and one day she said, "I don't really live here , I just come to work. My home is in Princeton. Would you like to come with me for the day—I'll pay your fare—because I'd like you to meet this famous person." She took a drawing from a sheaf and I recognised Einstein. Among the sheets were other faces I knew and I was thrilled.

"Would your mother let you go?"

"I think so," I said, knowing she would not.

"We could go on Saturday," she said. "On the train. You will like Princeton: it is beautiful."

I did not mention it to mother: I told her I was going to spend the day in the woods where I often went by myself to read.

This was the start of a wonderful day. Going by train was a thrill in itself; then we went to a big, light apartment, which she rented for her family. On entering the drawing room I stopped, amazed, for she had a whole wall hung with different sketches of Einstein, and hundreds of studies of roses.

Impressed as I was by Einstein, I loved the roses. The room seemed bathed in them, beautiful, reflecting sun and shade, such subtle and delicate colours one could almost smell them. I had never seen such paintings. I remember full-blown roses in a green glass bowl, the water translucent around the stems and petals full of summer warmth.

We had tea then walked to a rambling, slightly dilapidated old house in an unkempt garden nearby. It looked lived-in and comfortable, and that was how it looked inside, too. The chairs were big and squashy, worn leather, faded curtains and carpets with rich colours, the sort that grow mellow with age. Then Einstein walked in. I was shocked, partly at being in the presence of so great a man and partly because he looked so amazingly like the cartoon absent-minded professor. His wild, white hair stood up all over his head; on one foot he wore a sneaker and on the other a shoe; his shirt was collarless and the rest of his clothes looked as if they had been picked at random from a lucky dip. He seemed rather preoccupied. He shook hands with me and offered us tea but we did not stay rather to my relief and returned to the apartment, then took the train home.

I would love to have told mother but dared not. I was by now used to the pendulum swing of life, from happiness to fear but the next phase took me by surprise.

It was winter again .The weather had turned cold and thin snow was falling on the day mother had a letter from the sheriff saying that our house and everything in it was to be sold to cover debts (the house and debts belonged to father) and naming the day and hour of our eviction.

Mother was frantic. Bailiffs called and told her she could take all she could pack, but everything else had to be left and sold with the house.

Luckily just two weeks earlier she had sold the piano to her mother who paid in cash. The neighbours heard what was to happen and were indignant. They knew mother was in fragile health and had four children, the youngest only six years old. They remonstrated with the sheriff's men and tried to stop them coming into the house, then they rang the newspapers who sent a photographer to take pictures of us weeping and being put out on the pavement in the snow with nothing but our suitcases.

Then our neighbours called the police, who came but said it was the law and they could do nothing about it. The bailiffs had a writ. We were helpless. Dusk was falling as we stood in the street in the falling snow, four homeless children and their betrayed mother, a gift to the newspaper photographers, and one of the policemen said we had better go with him to the station. Did we have a family to contact? "You must have a family," he said to mother. She gave him her mother's address in Montrose Street, quite near to where we had lived in Hicks Street.

"You'll have to sleep in the police station tonight, and we'll take you to your mother's tomorrow," the policeman said, and took us off.

There was a big room for prisoners upstairs in the station. Just two beds, no covers, and some hard chairs. It was cold and in the night we could hear mice scurrying about. Between them and the children crying it was a terrible night. In the morning we got dressed and washed and they drove us to grandmother's. And then, in the warmth and comfort of her cramped house, secure in her love and care, the sun started to shine again.

# Chapter 11

My tall, straight grandmother stood on the doorstep, the wind ruffling her dark hair, arms open wide and we ran from the police car to her embrace. It was a long time since we had seen her, and her face folded in smiles as she hugged us and helped to drag the suitcases inside, up the stairs to the big bedroom, which we four sisters and mother were to share. The two little ones were to sleep in the big bed with mother; Marie and I had narrow trestles.

Grandmother and grandpa had moved out to the only other bedroom which was barely big enough to take their double bed and living quarters were cramped. This was not like upmarket Drexel Park. The neighbours were more like those we had had in Hicks Road, which was nearby: rougher, mainly first generation, some illiterate and most of them speaking poor English mixed with Italian. Some of them were from Naples and rumoured to be crooks. By contrast we were now "gentile" which in the street vernacular meant "stuck up". Mother was irritable and resentful and made it clear more than once a day to her own mother that she was used to a much higher standard of living.

Grandmother was a very tidy person and she gave each of us jobs to do. My daily task was to polish the brass doorknob and bell pull and scrub the stone step, rubbing it with pumice to make it white. My mother had to do the washing because it was too much for grandmother and there was no machine. There were two big washtubs in the room next to the kitchen. Grandmother did the cooking.

We four children (and I revelled in the freedom to be a child again) were happy with the change, especially when we smelled the delicious aroma of grandmother's cooking rise from the kitchen.

I missed the little farms and countryside of Drexel Park, the lovely gardens and the wildlife, but even as I think back, it is the winter warmth of meals in grandmother's kitchen that I remember best. The absence of hunger was a positive experience we no longer took for granted. As mother was not interested in cooking and even in the prosperous days could never be bothered to do much, this was the first time we had the sort of nourishing peasant food that was part of our Italian inheritance.

Grandmother stuffed artichokes. She bought dried cod, stiff with salt, soaked it for hours under cold running water and baked it in tomato and onion sauce. She made fresh pasta and meatballs fragrant with herbs. And she baked her own bread, kneading, stretching and slapping the dough, putting it to rise under a cloth by the stove, and bringing forth like magic from the oven loaves so crusty and soft I have never to this day tasted better.

Grandpa's wine from the cellar always accompanied grandmother's cooking. There was a cellar under the house with a dirt floor like the one we had in Hicks Street, but unlike father who put the goat in ours, grandfather had coal and wine in his. The wine, which he made himself, was lined up along one wall in barrels with wooden taps, and grandfather had to go down often to test it, which upset grandmother because he used to come up tipsy and feeling very jolly.

There was safety in grandmother's arms. She was affectionate and she was clever; she read the newspapers, knew the political issues of the day and took a lead in fighting for women's suffrage. But it was grandfather who made us laugh. He was shorter than his wife, thin and wiry, and had brilliant blue eyes. He also had the Lauria nose, which is very big.

He told us lots of stories about when he was a boy, and how his brother Nicholas ran away from home when he was ten years old, and earned his own living playing the violin in the streets and farmhouses of Pennsylvania until after months of searching, his distraught parents found him and took him home.

Grandpa also played the violin and had been a professional in a big orchestra, before rather to everyone's disappointment, he took a job in a small factory. He played his violin for us many an evening and when mother was in a good mood she would accompany him on the piano. Mother's brother, also called Nicholas used to stay with his parents from time to time when his work as a government surveyor took him in their direction. While we were there he slept on a divan in the sitting room. As the house now contained two pianos and he too was an accomplished musician, mother, Nicholas and grandfather would fill the house in the evening with music and singing.

Those were the good days. Uncle Nicholas was kind and clever. He was a graduate from Harvard University but he had had to change his name from Laurio to Larry to get in because of prejudice against Italians. He bought me books about art and discussed them with me and looked at my drawings. At Christmas he bought each of us children a pair of shoes.

Under my grandmother's care, our faces filled out. We did well at school, caught up with our lessons and made friends.

We went to the convent school around the corner where the nuns were kind and understanding and gave me special coaching to catch up because I had missed so much schooling.

One of the things I liked about grandmother's house was that the street was lined with trees. Across the road instead of houses there was a big church with a basilica and dome called

Santa Maria Magdelena della Pieta which became the first Italian Catholic cathedral in America. Between its paved precinct and the street were black ornate railings about five foot high and birds used to perch on them. I loved to sit at our front window, especially in winter when it snowed, looking at the soft light from the street gas lamps catching the flakes as they fell, and the black birds on the black railings behind. Beside the church was the convent and one wintry day when the snow was blowing down in sharp twirling gusts I saw the nuns come out of the convent two by two in their long habits, heads bent under black cowls, and the birds behind them huddled on the railings. As usual I had my drawing book with me so I hurriedly sketched them, and as often happened the image so imprinted itself in my memory that I can see them still.

From the house on foggy nights we could hear the boats on the Schuylkill River. Freight trains clanked in to the terminus from distant places like Texas and Ohio and tramps who stowed away for a free ride from state to state in their search for work would be chased off by the police and they slept in derelict warehouses along the riverside. Now bereft of Indian Basin for my solitary walks I used to wander to the riverside, slipping off when grandmother did not notice because she thought it was not safe in the Depression.

The church was a central part of her life. Every evening she went to benediction, a short service usually attended by the old women of the parish. The men did not go. We could hear the singing from our house: sweet, familiar cadences, which for my sisters and me were part of the comfort and security of being children in our grandparents' care. After the service the women, usually about ten of them, would stand under the gaslight, heads together, talking to grandmother who was much liked and respected.

The convent school for about 700 pupils—girls up to 17 and small boys—was on the other side of the church. I went in at the eighth grade but had missed so much that although I could read and write, I could not do even simple arithmetic and knew very little about other subjects that were a normal part of the curriculum.

Sister Agnita became my friend and mentor and when I was confirmed I took her name. She understood my problems and gave me extra help after school, especially in mathematics, so I caught up and started to do well. At the end of the year I won the top prize for "scholastic excellence"—a big gold-coloured medal showing a young girl holding the American flag and "For God and country" written on it. It was presented by one of the school governors, who was the very man my grandmother had wanted my mother to marry. He was by now an established lawyer, retiring in nature as my mother had been, and still unmarried. As he handed me the medal from the platform on prize giving day, he bent down and murmured in my ear, "You are the daughter I should have had." I think he loved my mother still.

She on the other hand still proclaimed at frequent intervals that she had a husband whose job was to look after her and her family, and she would not live like a beggar and supplicant. Father had not been in touch once during the whole year so at her brother's urging, mother went to court in Philadelphia to find him and make him pay for our support. The court authorities said that he was living outside the State so they could do nothing.

Mother brooded and spent most of the day by herself in our cramped bedroom. She was depressed. Her brother Nicholas realised she was on the edge of mental collapse and being a man of his time told her to "pull yourself together and look after the children." We had an allowance from the Family Welfare which had been notified by our former neighbours in Drexel Park after we were evicted and we lived rent free with grandmother. But now in her unsettled despair and feeling daily humiliated mother wanted to move. We wanted to stay.

The advantages of living where we now were seemed overwhelming to me though no one could deny it was extremely cramped, and for grandmother especially, having mother under the same roof was like living with an unexploded shell.

My sisters were all doing well at school and they blossomed, giggling and playing like other children their age, gaining confidence as well as weight.

Near the church, in Catherine Street, there was a community centre where we could learn typing and the piano and it was all free if you lived in the area. I started learning to type. Even better there was an art school where one could do a foundation course. It was run by two Catholic Germans, Mr Fleischman who was one of the founders, and Mr Gotliebe, an art teacher. I longed to go. I went and asked at the office and they told me there was a place available on the course, and quoted the fee. "But I haven't any money," I said. The administrator said to bring in a sample of my work and maybe some arrangement could be made.

I went home and did a pencil portrait of a film star, Billie Dove, which I copied from a photograph in a magazine and added two charcoal sketches and took them in. Mr Gotliebe looked at them, handed them back with a smile and said yes, he would award me one of the scholarships they kept for students without money. I ran home with the good news and started next day, an hour after school twice a week and all day Saturday. We did charcoal sketches of busts and casts of an ear, hands and feet, then life classes, and for most of the year I absorbed the delights of a world I hoped would become part of my whole life.

It did, but not yet. For now mother was determined to move from the sheltering parental home and find independence again. I pleaded with her. "We're doing well here, mother. Look how happy Dolly and Marcella are. And Maria has hardly been ill at all."

"I don't like it here," she said. In truth, it was too cramped and she knew we were a strain on her parents. Although my sisters and I with typical childhood resilience had quickly recovered from the trauma of the past, mother had not. She had a final quarrel with grandmother, accusing her of trying to turn the children against her, packed our bags, and we left.

My sisters and I were tearful. Grandmother was angry. Grandfather was upset as he helped carry the suitcases. "Where are you going?" grandmother demanded. "I'm concerned for the children. You're dumping all your problems on Nancy. She's too young for so much responsibility…"

She spoke to deaf ears. Mother had some Family Allowance money and a small sum her brother had given her to buy things for the children and she had found two rooms to rent near the High School in south Philadelphia.

Grandfather trundled up the threadbare stairs with our suitcases. It was cold. One room contained a stove and a cot and the other had three beds. It was without charm or cheer and our money ran out after two months. When we had no more for rent the landlady showed us the door and we trekked down the street with our suitcases to a boarded-up basement, which was condemned and gutted inside. We pulled off some of the boards, managed to get inside and became squatters.

# Chapter 12

For two days we stayed in the basement. We had water and candles and some bread but nothing else. I lit the candles and tried to start a fire in the rusty old stove for it was icy cold but everything was so damp, matches would not ignite the kindling.

"Couldn't we go back to grandmother's?" I begged mother, but she refused. I do not know what we would have done had we not been seen and heard by people who lived a few doors away. They called the police who arrived to evict us and this time drove us straight to the police station and contacted Family Aid.

Only when you are beaten to the ground as we were, do such organisations with their eternal begging bowls and appeals for funds assume the form of an efficient and benevolent, if slightly bossy, saviour.

Family Aid came in the shape of two sensibly-dressed middle-aged women to see mother. They signed us up to receive a weekly allowance and gave mother a small sum to tide her over. They served us a hot meal. And they gave us warm clothes, not just jumble but beautiful dresses donated by wealthy families in Philadelphia who were their main supporters. Best of all, they found us a place to live.

It was in Mrs Spinelli's house. Mrs Spinelli had a big house in Broad Street and had been quite wealthy but lost all except her home in the Depression. Her son lived with her and had a job and she made a small income by letting off two rooms on the third floor with use of the bathroom down the hall and gas hotplate for cooking. She also rented the second floor to a married couple who shared the bathroom and cooking facilities with us.

Mrs Spinelli was a nice, kind woman but she did not waste good money heating the house. Being too hot in summer and freezing in winter is one of the main trials of poverty and for us, shivering with cold had become the norm. The comfort of grandmother's house was already a fading dream when once again despite mother's truculence, her family came to the rescue.

This time it was Great Aunt Rose: the same one to whom mother had fled when she ran away to marry father and who had arranged—to grandmother's chagrin—a respectable wedding from her own house. Grandfather, her brother must have contacted her.

I liked Aunt Rose on sight. Mother, predictably, did not want to see her. Eating humble pie was not to her taste, and although nobody reminded her of it, her marital mistake hung in the air.

Rose had a happy and forgiving nature. She had come to help and that was what she was going to do, sweeping away mother's objections with one of her favourite sayings: "there's an answer to every problem".

She had been married 35 years to John Borneo, 18 years of them childless, before to their great joy and surprise they had a son. Anthony was now 18, a year older than me, and he became my friend and companion.

Rose's arrival brought hope and some fun into our lives. She had vivid blue eyes like grandfather's, his pale blonde hair and what women's magazines in those days called a "plump" figure—as if she cared. She would have called herself short and rather curvy and laughed till the curvy bits wobbled.

She did not have much money and Uncle John did not make much in his unglamorous job running a small employment agency for barbers but that did not bother her either. My great grandfather who had been so anxious to educate his four sons had not really counted girls in the academic stakes though Rose, with her brothers and sister Anna, learned to play a musical instrument. Like many fathers of his day great grandfather thought that as girls got married and had families rather than jobs, it was better to leave them money and property. Most of the money Aunt Rose was left had been lost in the Depression when the banks collapsed, but she still had three little houses in Philadelphia which she rented out and a rambling house by the sea in Ocean City which she would rent in the summer while she moved into the attic.

At the time she came into our lives, the tenants in her houses had lost their jobs and did not have the money to pay, so typically, Rose told them they could stay rent free if they would just pay the tax on the properties which amounted to about $30 a year.

"Never mind, we can manage," I heard her declare more than once. It was another of her "sayings". "There's a good meal on the table and here we are all together and the more the merrier, thanks be to our Blessed Mother of Jesus." She was very religious, a catholic of course; generous and optimistic, and I learned a lot from her. "Never be petty," she taught us. "If you step on every stone in life you'll never get to where you want to go."

Mother was still stepping on every stone, resentful of everyone in the family whom she blamed for "letting her down". That did not deter Rose in the least. "It doesn't matter," she said to me. "Now don't worry because I'm coming in the old Buick with Anthony to see you again and I'm bringing some of my soup", and she would turn up with it from her house in

Philadelphia, sometimes with pasta and meat balls and lots of bread.

My three sisters and I often went to her house for meals and Rose loved having family all around. "The more the merrier," she'd say happily, dolloping out pasta at least three times a week. I met cousins I'd never seen before, and members of the family I'd never heard of. No matter who turned up, Rose was happy to feed them. She fussed over Marcella who was now seven years old, and lively Dolly with the bouncing brown curls, and did her best to bolster Marie's frail health with wholesome food. For me, her home was a sanctuary where some evenings I could get away from mother who was becoming ever more unreasonable and depressed.

As much as mother distrusted strangers, Rose loved to have her house full of young people. Her son Anthony was popular and outward-going like his mother, so it was nothing for her to have six young men and a few of their girlfriends in her house for coffee and doughnuts in the evenings. Anthony used to fetch me in the Buick. I loved meeting his friends, the excitement of chatting to handsome young men, the even greater excitement of kissing them in the vestibule (the game was called "postman's room" and involved calling numbers and kissing the girl or boy if you got the right one) while Great Aunt Rose, a silent but vigilant chaperon sat on the sofa doing her crochet and pretending to take no notice.

In summer she drove us to her house by the sea, about 60 miles away, a journey that took a couple of hours in the car going through beautiful countryside. Sometimes we went by train to spend week ends when the weather was good. Mother always stayed at home.

This was a strange period of sparkling light and deep darkness in my life. I felt the optimism and pent-up excitement of youth, when everything seems possible and on your side. I knew I looked attractive. Young men eyed me as I walked by, and I covertly looked at them. I imagined myself becoming a great artist and travelling the world, and Aunt Rose with her pasta and her laughter made all of it seem normal.

Then I would go home to our two rooms and mother. We were hard up and when Rose was not coming to the rescue, usually hungry. Our rooms were clean but there was not enough space and no heating. But the worst thing was mother's desperation. I think she was moving towards madness. The contrast between her formerly comfortable and even rich life and her present poverty filled her with bitter humiliation and indignation. "Why don't you get a job?" she railed at me. "You don't care if we starve. You should be earning money."

"But I can't find a job. I've tried. There isn't any work," I tried to explain.

"You could beg in the streets."

"No, mother!" I protested. "No, I couldn't do that."

"If you love me you will," she screamed, bringing out the old blackmail phrase. "If you love me you'll go out and bring home the money to buy us food."

My resolve collapsed. Feeling miserably ashamed and hoping nobody I knew would see me, I went to the entrance of the subway, and held out my bowl. People walked briskly past. Some glanced down and moved on showing the mixture of guilt and annoyance people feel when they are asked for money by a beggar when everyone is having a hard time. A few threw nickels into my bowl and I muttered my thanks. In all the day I only made $2 and it cost me my pride.

As darkness fell I went home and handed over the money. I was humiliated and angry. "I shall never do that again mother," I said. "Never, whatever happens. There's no work here. I'm going away to find a job. I'll send you all the money I can as soon as I find something, and it will be money I've earned."

My plan was to go to New York. There was bound to be work there, some job I could do, however menial. Aunt Rose had a sister called Anna who lived in Harlem. She was a widow, as dark as Rose was fair, with the same dumpy figure, keen sense of humour and generosity, but a far better sense of business.

She needed it. Her husband, a builder, had been killed in a tragic accident leaving her suddenly alone with two children to bring up. The girl, Kate was now grown up and married, but Anna's son who was in his late teens had leukaemia and lived at home. Anna made a living renting out houses she had bought during more prosperous days in Harlem, letting to mainly black tenants. I would write to Anna and ask if I could stay with her while I found my feet and work in the big city.

First I needed to earn the fare. It cost $3 to get to New York by subway. I scanned the adverts and saw a live-in job as a cleaner, food and a bed included. The wage was just enough: $3 a week. The hours were long and the work hard, but it was the first step and I wrote at once to Great Aunt Anna.

By return of post I had a letter back: "Yes, come as soon as you finish work on Saturday," she said. "I'll meet you at the station. I'll be there, waiting." The same day I rang the woman at Family Welfare and told her what I was doing and asked her to keep an eye on mother. I knew her quite well by now and she understood my problems. I could be more use to mother sending her a weekly supplement and Marie was old enough, and by now fit enough, to help in the house. I left them Anna's address in case of emergencies, then at the end of the week I stuffed my few clothes into a bag , my $3 wages into my pocket and went down to the subway to get the train.

On the journey, looking out of the windows at the green countryside of Pennsylvania slipping past I felt excited at the prospects opening up. I knew it would be tough. Millions of people were looking for work. But I would do anything legal and I had the security of being with Aunt Anna.

She was there on the station to meet me just as she said she would. I was tall and thin; she was short and round like Rose—and we hugged each other laughing, on my side with relief at having escaped from home and found a safe haven.

We walked to the house chatting as we went. Her house was one in a row, railings in front, steps up to the front door, a shining brass knocker. Anna, the woman of property, wore a big bunch of keys round her waist and she took one now to let us in. Down the stairs to meet us came her son Bobby, a sweet-natured boy, so thin and tired with his fatal illness it broke my heart to see him. He kept racing pigeons in a loft at the top of the house; tagged their legs and sent them on journeys he could never make himself to fly home free, circling the huge city and down to his little loft with clean sawdust on the floor and tin bowls of corn.

Anna never put the tragedies of her life on show. She was resourceful, matter-of-fact, and she could be tough. She was well known in the neighbourhood and although she was the rent-collector, smiles and waves of the hand greeted her as she went on her rounds. "Come with me, Nan," she said, and I went willingly to explore the streets. Harlem was a mixed area, black and white, some workless men sitting about aimlessly, women chatting in groups, children playing on the sidewalks as we had in Hicks Street. Some of Anna's tenants could not pay the rent. I listened with interest to how she handled each situation: sometimes the tough landlady with a pay-up-or-go ultimatum, sometimes sympathetic: "Well pay me when you can manage it."

Rose, I reflected, would have let them all off. Anna explained. "I know who is putting it on and who is genuine. Some of those rascals can find the money easily enough when it comes to a packet of cigarettes or a tot of bootleg so why should I let them live rent-free? I need the money too."

Anna set no limit on my stay. I think she was glad of the company and there was plenty of room in her house. But I had to get a job fast. On Monday morning I took the subway to Times Square where there was a huge Woolworth's. When I was at school I had worked in a Woolworth's on Saturdays, so I had the magic ingredient, "experience". "Sorry," the manager said. "We've got nothing. Try Play Brothers. They are just across the square."

I did. They were shut. I banged on the door. "Sorry, we're shut," someone shouted.

"I'm desperate," I yelled back through the door. "I've got to get work. I used to work in Woolworths...."

The door opened and a woman stood there. "Yes?" she said. "Well they need a girl at the fountain. Perhaps you'd do. " She made a telephone call. "Yes, you'll do. A week's trial to start. Nine dollars a week, six days and 12 hours on Saturdays. And you get a free lunch." It worked out about 25 cents and hour.

"I'll take it," I said. There were three other girls there and we got on well together. I registered for some free state-run art classes in the evening though I was usually too tired to go to them and I managed to send a few dollars to mother every week. Things, I thought were getting better. I looked out for a more highly-paid job or at least one with shorter hours so that I could spend more time on art classes. Six months went by. Then I had a letter from the Family Welfare officer.

"You must come home as soon as possible," she said. "Your mother is in very bad shape and I'm afraid for your two youngest sisters. They need your help."

My heart sank—but what could I do? With reluctance Anna agreed: I had no choice. So I packed my bag again and took the $3 subway journey back to Philadelphia, back to the anguish and crises of life with mother.

# Chapter 13

Mrs Spinelli let me in at the front door and I climbed the stairs wearily to our second floor rooms wondering what I would find. When mother opened the door I could see from her look of suspicion, swiftly followed by an expression of belligerence as she recognised me, that nothing had changed for the better: if anything, it was worse.

She was not pleased to see me.

"Hello mother," I said, and went to kiss her. She turned her face away but my two little sisters stopped playing and ran to me. Mother said angrily, "You deserted us! You left us without anything to live on and now you walk back as if nothing happened. I'll never forgive you." She was as good as her word. She never did.

I tried to say, "But I sent you money every week." It made no difference.

There was the same cold, the same threadbare poverty, the rooms clean but empty of comfort and worst of all the constant fear that anything however innocently intended could ignite an explosion of rage from mother.

Despite all this there was, outside on the streets, a feeling of optimism like the first smells of spring, for the country's economy had started to show some signs of recovery. Real recovery did not come until industry was stimulated by the demands of war, but the new president, Franklin Roosevelt was organising a programme to give food vouchers for the destitute and to create jobs through new programmes of work.

I registered with the WPA—the Works Progress Administration—for work, and mother and I registered for relief cheques. It took us four days to get anything because the offices were makeshift and there were hundreds of people in the line. On arrival we were given a number, after which we sat on benches and waited.

Eventually we had our stamps, which entitled us to tins of food like bully beef that we could mix with potatoes, and rice, butter, milk, sugar and flour and even some fruit. We were also given shoes—heavy and ungainly, but they kept our feet dry— and $10 a week for the rent.

Meanwhile my sisters went to school and I sought work, but with little success. Mother's outbursts of anger were becoming more uncontrollable and she often attacked me physically, dragging me by my long hair while she shouted and accused. In the midst of this I started to get terrible abdominal pain. I would have tried to ignore it but the pain was too intense and Mrs Spinelli called the doctor. He diagnosed appendicitis and said an operation would be necessary.

"I can't help that. I haven't got any money," mother said.

"She'll die without one," the doctor warned "She's got to go to hospital, and straight away. I'll arrange it." He did. He contacted the woman from Family Aid and I was taken to the Catholic hospital of St Agnes. Mother came too.

They put me into a ward with other women where I was tucked under the rough white sheets by a sympathetic nurse who told me not to worry. My forehead was damp with the pain. Mother stood watching. Suddenly from the other side of the ward a voice called out, "Well if it isn't Tessie! Hello! I am glad to see you again, and such a long time it has been! What are you doing here?"

Mother froze. She would not turn round or reply. Instead she glared at me. The woman, I think, was a relative of my father's but I am not sure. Mother hissed at me, "You knew she was here! You planned it. It was a trick to make me see her."

"But I don't know who she is, mother," I whispered. "I've never seen her." But mother had turned on her heels and walked out. I cried miserably as she left without a backward glance and I did not see her again until three weeks after the operation.

I had surgery and returned to the ward. And there I stayed, and stayed, unvisited—until eventually the medical staff said they could not afford to keep me any longer and contacted mother to take me home.

I was dressed and waiting on a chair in the hospital corridor when she came to pick me up. Her expression was icy. I was physically weak and tried to smile as I held on to her arm for support and walked slowly from the hospital. Mother had cut herself off from all her family; she would not speak to her own mother, nor let her see the children. She brooded silently as if she were looking into an alien and threatening world that had no link with the real world around her. In her mind I had become part of the conspiracy against her.

At home I was still too weak to work. Most of the day I sat drawing in my sketchbook and keeping out of mother's way. In her fantasy world she was persuading herself that I had not had an operation at all, that I was making it all up. "But mother, see for yourself," I said, lifting my dress to bare the stitched-up wound on my abdomen. Mother's face contorted with fury. She raised her clenched fist and brought it down with all her strength on to the cut and a spurt of blood ran out as stitches tore apart. I shouted with the pain and Mrs Spinelli ran upstairs to see what had happened.

"Nan's fallen and hurt herself," mother said quickly. I said nothing but I felt the tears run down my cheeks and the burning pain.

"You must go back to hospital. Something's gone wrong," Mrs Spinelli said, pretending to believe mother. "I'll take you."

At the hospital the doctor was puzzled. "I can't understand it. How did this happen?"

"I fell and hit myself on the edge of the table," I lied.

The doctor repaired the stitches. "Take care this time," he said.

"And how can I do that," I wondered to myself as Mrs Spinelli took me home in a taxi. Mother opened the door. She smiled at me, and looked concerned. She realised what she had done and I could see she was sorry. For a short while, she reverted to the kind and shy mother I remembered in my distant childhood, when she would pile up her auburn hair and put a pretty hat on top to go out in father's red car.

It did not last.

I sat drawing in my book where I kept sketches of my friends, and banking on mother's new-found mellowness I asked her if I could do her portrait.

"Why, yes Nan," she said agreeably. She posed while I drew.

Next day she said, "Why did you want that drawing of me? What's behind it?"

"Nothing, mother. I just wanted a picture of you."

"Give me the book," she demanded.

"No mother…"

She glanced towards the drawer where it was kept. I knew she would tear it up and I dashed to get hold of it first then I ran to the window and threw it out.

This, I think, was when I realised mother really was mad. In a wild fury she flung herself at me, biting and scratching my face and arms with her nails, tearing at my hair, ripping my dress. Her eyes were wide and glaring, her hair tangled and hanging around her face and she seemed to be attacking some demon that terrified her with a fury beyond her normal strength.

In my nightmare dreams I had seen this scene. Mrs Spinelli was out visiting her sister. I was trapped in the room where there were two beds (we slept three to a bed) and two doors, one leading to the hall, and one of the beds was jammed against the other door to save space. I dashed to the hall door and mother did too. She had a long pair of scissors in her hand. I went to the other door, pushed the bed out of the way and shoved it against the other wall squashing mother behind it, and made my escape.

I stumbled down the stairs holding up my torn slip with one hand and ran into the street. It was snowing, I was freezing and bleeding from long scratches on my face and arm , standing on the steps outside and crying hysterically. Mother stood by the door and shouted, "You can't come in. You can stay there till I fetch you in…"

I forgot about the sketchbook. I ran from the door, still more terrified of mother than of the frozen street. But then I heard Mrs Spinelli's voice. She had come home. She was standing by the door, speaking to mother.

"I don't know what's the matter with Nan," I heard mother saying to her. "She is acting in such a strange way. She's been following me around and watching me. I think there is something wrong with her."

Mrs Spinelli got the picture. She had heard the commotion, mother screaming at me and saw my tears. She pretended to believe my mother.

"You go upstairs Mrs Circelli," she said. "I'll deal with your daughter. I'll see she doesn't bother you any more." She glared at me. "Come on." Mother slowly climbed back upstairs to her own rooms and Mrs Spinelli took my arm with mock roughness and ushered me into her kitchen.

"We have to get your mother into hospital," she said gently when we were alone. "She has a mental problem. We can do nothing about it; it is nothing to do with you. She is ill and she needs the help of doctors."

"But she would never go," I said.

"We will have to call the police," she said. "They'll know how to do it."The police came in a red emergency car. They spoke briefly with Mrs Spinelli downstairs, then went up to mother and told her that they were going to take her to Bibury Hospital for a rest and observation for a few days. Bibury was the city mental hospital in Philadelphia. I do not know how the police persuaded mother to go with them, but she put together a small bag with her toilet things, got into the car and they drove off while I waited terrified in Mrs Spinelli's kitchen.

When she had gone, Mrs Spinelli asked, "Now what will you and your sisters do? Have you got some relatives to go to?"

"I'll call Aunt Rose," I said. And like the practical and willing ally she had always been, Rose took us all in to her own small house and looked after us.

A few weeks later, feeling worried about mother I went to Bibury Hospital to visit her and see what was happening. It was noisy, overcrowded and smelly. Mother was in a big ward that seemed to be full of women crying, babbling, some of them screaming, one woman defecating in the corner, and one I saw holding a doll she thought was her baby. And there was my poor mother cowering in a corner.

"Oh Nan," she pleaded, "I'm better now. I'm all right now. You can take me home. Look at me—you can see I'm better. Please take me with you."

I did not believe she was better, yet I would have rescued her from that place if I could. But I was under age. They could not release her to me.

I took the bus back to Rose's house with a heavy heart. Once there, the business of life took over. Rose had rented out her beach house for the summer, so we stayed in a smaller one nearby, which was really too cramped for us all, but we managed and were happy to be free of the tensions of the last months. My youngest sisters went to school, Maria who was now nearly 17 helped to look after them and I found a job as waitress in a small restaurant on the beach.

It was a good restaurant owned by two sisters who were smart and educated. One of them taught me how to wait at the tables, and I earned $8 a week, which was not much, but the tips were good.

It was not very long before, thanks to the tips, I had saved up enough money to rent a flat for my sisters and myself in Winton Street, near to Rose's house. It did not cost much. There were two little bedrooms, a kitchen and bathroom, a few easy chairs and a radio—one of the nicest places we had lived in since we were evicted from Drexel Park. We still had some help from Family Aid to supplement my wages and for a few months life became quite normal.

Maria looked after the two little ones, getting them off to school and collecting them afterwards and she kept house for us all. I found a new, better-paid job in a cafeteria as a "bus girl", which means I picked up the dishes from the counter, delivered them to the tables and cleared them away afterwards. Meanwhile a friend tipped me off about a government-sponsored job—the Museum Expansion Project it was called—where there was to be work for artists building educational models in the city museum. Applicants had to get their names down on the list for an appointment for interview, which would turn up at some unspecified date, and if you missed it you lost your chance. So I put my name on the list and for the moment forgot about it.

# Chapter 14

I liked working at the cafeteria but there were problems. These were caused by my being 18 years old and having a good figure, and the cook thinking he was irresistible to women. Like many men who worked in cafeterias at this time he was a drifter going from state to state and he usually turned up for work drunk, which might have accounted for his Romeo complex. His name was Jarvis.

Jarvis did some winking and nudging and when I took no notice, he started telling the others I was frigid. "Watch out for him. He's going to try and get you," Christina warned me. She was a tall, blonde Swedish waitress and we were friends. Christina was even more streetwise than I, and she was protective towards me. So one night, when I was on the late shift and so was Jarvis who showed up inebriated as usual, Christina dropped around because, she said, she had forgotten something. Which was lucky for me.

In cafeterias where staff worked late shifts it was mandatory to have a rest room with a sofa or a bed in it and Jarvis had a plan to lock me in the rest room with himself for sole company. He had just about managed it, with me shouting and trying to stop him locking the door when Christina charged in to the rescue, socked him one and made such a din that the rest of the staff came running in. What with the alcohol and the beating Jarvis must have had a sore head the next day.

The incident cemented a firm friendship between Christina and me. But Christina was in trouble herself. She was pregnant and the father of her child was a married man whose wife was in a sanatorium. He could not marry her although they loved each other and Christine felt she could not go to her family for help because of the disgrace in those days of having a child outside marriage. "I can't tell them, Nan," she said. "But I can manage, I'm sure I can. Ralph will pay for my lodgings and I love him so much."

Today when so many children are born to single parents Christine's predicament may not seem much of a problem, but then it took a brave woman to follow that path alone. Christine was brave and strong—but not physically. In childhood she had had rheumatic fever and it left her with a weak heart. Now in pregnancy she was losing strength and her deteriorating heart was to blame.

"I'll find you a room near our apartment and I will look after you," I said. Her lover said he would pay for her food and rent, so we found a little place and I used to call in every day and cook her a meal and get what she needed. But to my great distress I could see Christine getting weaker.

Marie was able to look after our young sisters at night, which freed me to take care of my beloved friend. She lay pale and limp on her bed, her lips and finger nails tinged with the tell-tale blue of a failing heart , but she would smile and speak cheerfully. "Nancy, when this is over I am going to take you out and buy you a beautiful outfit, and I will help you with your sisters", she said. But we both knew she was not likely to survive.

Ralph, her boyfriend was distraught. As she grew weaker I begged her to let me contact her mother.

"Yes", she conceded at last. "Yes…tell her I want to see her. And my aunt… a catholic like you, Nancy: a convert. I wish

I had your faith …I think I am going to die." she murmured. I wrote her out a pamphlet about the Immaculate Conception, which she said gave her comfort, and helped her to pray, and I contacted her mother.

Meanwhile the peace and security at our small flat was suddenly and completely destroyed by the unexpected arrival of my mother from the mental hospital.

I opened the door one evening and there she was on the doorstep, brought straight from the hospital by my grandmother who simply dumped her outside our house and drove away.

Maybe the love my grandmother still felt for her once most-favoured daughter had made it impossible for her to ignore Theresa's pleas to be released from Bibury Hospital even though she knew she could not care for mother herself. Or maybe it was the stigma that existed at that time against sickness of the mind that made her deny mother had any mental problems.

What I do know is that the loving grandmother who had given us a safe haven when we were evicted from Drexel Park now turned her back on us and blamed me for mother's commitment to a mental institution. She lived to regret it though she never faced me again. But my uncle told me that when she was dying of cancer several years later, grandmother said, "If only I could see Nan to tell her how wrong I was. I didn't help them when they needed me."

There was, in truth, no time when I needed help more, for now, with mother living with us I felt my two youngest sisters were in danger.

Yet she was still my mother and I loved her. She came in hesitantly and put her bag in a bedroom. "You see," she said, "I told you I was better." Marcella, now 10 years old, and Dolly, 13, put their arms round her, and we had supper together. "You shouldn't have sent me to that place," she said. "I will never go back. I won't leave this flat."

She meant it. She literally would not set foot outside, all through the hot and humid summer.

I gave up my job in the cafeteria and found work to do at home so that I could keep an eye on her. I became a jobber, smocking children's dresses. The man who employed the jobbers would bring me 100 dresses at a time, and I had to put four rows of smocking along each bodice top, for which I would be paid 20 cents a dress. It was hard work and not much money and he cheated me often but I was in no position to quit.

Maria only made $3 a week as a housemaid, but as she lived in she could spare us some of it. She was working very hard all hours, caring for little children so she was constantly on call for them, as well as doing all the housework. She was too tired to do anything for us at the end of the day. But Rose helped. She used to send her son, cousin Anthony around with soup and other food for us. He was very careful not to upset mother who tolerated him, I think, because he reminded her of Leonard. And Rose sent us clothes as well, which we cut down to fit and we had some more from a charity organisation and shoes, which meant I no longer had to wear my old ones with newspaper stuffed into them. Marie and I shared a pair of stockings. We took it in turns and when she went out to work, she wore them.

Despite all this, we would have managed all right if it were not for the fact that mother was paranoid, violent and getting worse, and I was terrified that she would harm my younger sisters.

Although I kept an eye on her, she managed one day to climb on to a ledge by the rooftop taking Marcella with her, and I heard her saying, "Now we are going to jump off together." I pulled Marcella back and mother after her. Mother complained, "You are always watching me, Nan. Stop spying on me. What is the matter with you?"

She kept herself clean but she had stopped bothering about her appearance. She looked wild and dishevelled, and sat for hours every day rocking on a chair by the window, terrified that if she moved someone would snatch her and put her back into the mental hospital. She watched me constantly and brooded.

When a man from a hostel nearby knocked at the door and asked me if I would take delivery of a parcel he was expecting from his family, mother heard and shouted, "Why are you here? What do you want? Go away! Get out! Get out!"

She was suspicious of everyone. I tried to explain to her but she was obsessed with her fears. She used to listen to the radio and think that the people speaking on it were after her and spying on her. One afternoon when I slipped out to see Christina—it was Maria's day off and she stayed at home—I got back to find mother trying to throw the radio out of the window. "That man has got no right to speak to me in that way," she was shouting while Maria tried to calm her.

"It was the programme..." Maria said, "the man was talking about the sort of skin he loves to touch ..."

"How dare he speak to me like that!" Mother was incensed and very noisy about it as Maria fielded the radio and put it in a safe place.

The landlord who lived downstairs was turning nasty. He was afraid of mother, perhaps because she was always shouting at him, "I know what you are up to" and worse. He wanted us all out. In the midst of all this I was doing my best to look after Christina, to cook her meals and bring her some comfort. I knew we could not go on like this. Mother was too unpredictable and I was afraid. I decided to go to Dr Melchiori who had been our family doctor for years.

Dr Melchiori was understanding and sympathetic.

"What can I do?" I asked. "What if she harms the children?" My youngest sister was only eight years younger than I, but after taking responsibility for the family for so long, I felt a generation older than Marcella and Dolly. They were still children. They had to be protected.

Dr Melchori sighed. "You could take her back to Bibury Hospital," he suggested. "They've got her records there."

"No, I can't do that. It was terrible. She was miserable and she is frightened of going back." I pleaded, "Don't you know of another hospital, a better one? Somewhere where she won't be unhappy?"

"There is the Norristown State Hospital," the doctor said. "It's very progressive, very modern in its approach. The grounds are really beautiful, like a park, and the patients are in small buildings that house groups with similar mental problems. It won't be like it was in Bibury. Your mother won't be with people who are worse than she is."

That sounded reasonable. "What should I do?" I asked. "How do we get her there?"

"It's a legal process," he said. "You must get an attorney and have her committed through the courts."

I left with plans going through my head. I couldn't find an attorney myself, but perhaps Rose could. Perhaps there was someone in the family who could help. Rose's brothers were doctors and one was a lawyer. I explained my fears to her. "We can't leave it: there will be a tragedy. It will be too late."

Rose agreed. She spoke to her brothers, and to grandmother, and their reaction was the same: "There's no insanity in this family. Theresa just has nerves; she's highly-strung. If the children behave properly she will be perfectly all right. Nancy just wants to be free to have a good time..."

"Well," said Rose, "we'll just have to manage on our own. I know a lawyer. He's a friend of mine. We'll go to see him."

We did, and I told him what had been happening. He was not encouraging. "It will take months to get to court," he said, "and from what you say, it can't wait. And there's another thing. Even if I waive my fee, the cost of going to court will be $100 to $150."

"So what can I do?"

" Getting it on to the judicial calendar is the most difficult bit. Perhaps the doctor can make them see it is urgent."

I went to the church around the corner and asked for guidance. Then I visited the Norristown State Hospital to look at it and was reassured by the sight of patients sitting in the sunshine in the gardens and the general appearance of uncrowded calm. I went back to Dr Melchiori.

"There is a way we could do it," he said, "but we'll have to get three doctors, and your local councillor to sign the papers. It's difficult. I'll have to get into your house and examine her, see how she behaves. Do you think you could persuade her to let me in?"

I said, "I'll get Marcella to pretend she is ill. I'll explain to her it's the only way of getting mother to see a doctor. Then if you ask mother where her husband is or something like that, it will set her off. "

We arranged a date. I went home and spoke to my youngest sister. "Look, Marcella, mother is not well, so I want you to pretend you have a stomach ache, a really bad one, and then she will let the doctor in and he can see how she is. He'd like to talk to her and give her some medicine. Will you do this for me?"

"Yes," she said.

Next, I rang the State Hospital and told them that Dr Melchiori wanted mother to go there. "If I have all the proper paperwork signed by the doctors and the committal from court, will you take her in? " I asked. They said they would. "Let us know when you are coming and we will be ready for you," the administrator said.

Next day Marcella complained about a terrible stomach ache. She groaned and writhed realistically and mother was very concerned.

"We must call the doctor, mother," I said. "I think she has got appendicitis .It seems like the sort of pain I had and it can be very dangerous."

"We don't need a doctor," mother said.

Another groan came from Marcella. "All right, you'd better call him," mother conceded.

Dr Melchiori came round at once. I answered the door. "I understand your daughter is not well," he said, addressing mother.

"You needn't come in," she said, "I'll send Marcella out to you."

Marcella uttered another groan. " I've got to come in right away," the doctor insisted, "it sounds to me as if she is very sick," and he pushed his way in.

Mother regretted it immediately. The doctor looked at Marcella, then he turned to mother and said, "And your husband?"—just like that. Mother went berserk. She attacked him, she accused him of plotting with her husband to frame her and get her sent away and she chased him out of the apartment.

"Definitely paranoid," Dr Melchiori said when I called him afterwards. "And I've got the reports from Bibury. I can get the other doctors to sign the forms for you. Come for the papers at the end of the week."

I did—and the next step was to get into the court and somehow jump the queue to get the committal order signed by a judge.

I went to the court house, into the room where they were hearing the cases and sat at the back of the room. When the last one was over and the bailiff was standing by the judge, I got up and ran forward, calling to the judge, "Help me, you must help me." The bailiff ran towards me to try and stop me as I called, "You must let me talk to you."

The judge said to the bailiff, "Wait, I'll hear what she says." I thrust the papers into his hand. "They are all signed," I said, "my mother is mentally ill, she's dangerous, she has to be committed, I want her to go to the Norristown State Hospital, I don't want her to go back to Bibury…"

The judge looked concerned and took the papers. He adjourned the court and spoke to two other judges, checked that the papers were in order and signed them. Then he handed them to me. "You're a brave little lady," he said, "and I wish you luck."

I knew that I would need it—and a good plan of action to get mother out of the house.

Dr Melchiori had made the arrangements for mother's admittance to Norristown State Hospital, but the institution's administrators explained that it was over the county border so we would have to take her in ourselves. This was going to be difficult—a 10 mile car drive and she was very suspicious. Despite the stifling, hot weather she had refused to go out since she arrived and the only person allowed over the threshold of our flat apart from my sisters and me was my cousin Anthony.

I had to find a way of getting her out and into Anthony's car—and fast.

# Chapter 15

Mother was sitting on the rocking chair by the window. To and fro she rocked, day after perspiring day, the monotonous sound of the rockers on wood the background to her weary, empty brooding. Cheap lace curtains filtered the sun but the heat was still stifling. She sighed, mopped her damp hair and tried to fan herself with a piece of paper.

The weather was perfect for my plan.

Mother used to love picnics. Perhaps we could get her out of the house on the pretext of going for a picnic by the stream in the countryside, tempt her with the thought of cool running water and a light breeze blowing through the trees. Ever suspicious and watchful, I knew she would not go with me. But if the children went too…

"It's such a hot day, I'm going to take Dolly and Marcella out for a picnic," I said to her. "Why don't you come too, mother? Anthony says he will drive us in the car to the country—Uncle John's lent him his old car to take us out. It would do you good to come with us. "Oh, come too," Dolly implored. "You never go anywhere with us now. Anthony's friend's coming too—that boy he knew at school."

I was putting some bread and cheese and a few apples into the picnic basket. I'd rung the hospital administrator to tell him we might be coming, that we would be there in an hour if we could.

"No, I'm afraid to go," mother said. "And I'm too tired." She would not budge.

So the rest of us went on the picnic, sat by the stream and paddled and ate our apples. It was a lovely afternoon and when Dolly and Marcella bounded back into the house they were full of chatter about what a good time they had had.

The following weekend I tried again. Another picnic. My sisters were ecstatic. I cut sandwiches, put some bottles of water and apples in the basket, and Andrew and his friend turned up in the car again.

"Will you come this time, mother?" I asked, trying to be casual, not to make her suspicious. The temperature was up in the nineties and in that airless little room mother sat on her chair by the window overlooking the dusty street, rocking and rocking. "No," she said. "I mustn't go out. I must stay here."

Again I rang the hospital administrator to say that our ruse had failed. Again the rest of us went on the picnic and afterwards the children went skipping home to tell mother what a lovely afternoon they had had.

I tried again. Aunt Rose came too with Anthony and his friend, and I rang the hospital: "We'll be there in an hour unless we ring you." Again I packed a picnic and Dolly and Marcella put in towels to dry their legs after paddling in the stream and told mother that she should come too.

"I'm tired," she said.

"Oh, mother..."

"Well perhaps...I'd love to get out for a bit..."

"You mustn't come if you would prefer not to," I said. "I don't want you to be worried ."

"But you will come, won't you mother," Marcella implored her. Mother smiled. "Well perhaps just this time. It's so hot. Yes, just this once. I'll put on another dress."

She got up from her rocking chair, put her purse on the cushion and went to the bathroom to wash and put on a clean dress.

While she was doing that I opened her purse and found a pair of scissors, so I took them out and hid them.

Mother emerged from the bathroom with her hair combed and wearing the clean dress. But she was still undecided. "I don't know…" she started.

"Oh, please mother," said Dolly, catching her hand.

"If you are worried mother, don't come," I said.

"Yes, I'll come," she said. She walked to the door and glanced back around the room. "I'll never see this place again," she said, half to herself. Was she suspicious? She spoke with certainty, yet calmness. And she walked out.

As we got into the car her unease returned. She stepped back, glanced over her shoulder and moved away. Anthony's friend said, "Come on, it's getting late; we ought to go." If he had been a man she would have refused to get in, but he was just a boy. I jumped in quickly after her and Anthony started up the car. We hadn't gone three blocks before mother demanded to be taken home. "I don't want to go on," she screamed. "Let me get out and she struggled to get at the doors. But Anthony had taken off the door handles. Mother grabbed her purse, opened it and looked for the scissors, but I had taken them. She shouted, struck out and Marcella started crying. "What's the matter, mummy?"

Mother threw her purse at Anthony's head and tried to snatch his hands off the steering wheel, and the boy and I held her arms down and tried to calm her. We still had a long way to go. She was so strong, she kicked and shouted and the two children were sobbing and screaming to her to stop. Mothers dress was torn and she was soaked in perspiration, her hair bedraggled, eyes wild. Anthony kept his eyes on the road, driving as fast as he could, weaving his way through the traffic, his hand down on the horn, up the driveway to the hospital, left to the block where the administrator had told us he would have staff waiting.

They were there. By this time mother was exhausted. She had a terrible, haunted look in her eyes: betrayed, angry, defeated, and resigned. Her hair was soaked and hanging round her face and her dress was ripped. The children were crying hysterically. They did not understand what was happening and hung on to me as I, sobbing as well, climbed out of the back of the car.

One of the hospital men opened the door for mother and took her arm as she tried to make a run for it. I saw her head and shoulders sag as he started to lead her to the building. She was beaten, finished, and she knew it. But as she passed me, she pulled her arm free and slapped me across the face as hard as she could and said with bitter hate, "I never want to see you again as long as I live." She hit me so hard that her bracelet fell off, but it was not the physical pain that made me weep.

I put my two sisters in the car and tried to console them and explain that our mother was not well. Then wet with my own tears I went with the psychiatrist, a big, kind woman, to sort out the papers. "I had to do it; I had to do it," I kept repeating. "I didn't know what else to do." The doctor said, "You did the right thing. Don't go home and think about what your mother said. She's ill. Come back in six weeks and she will be different. She'll be over the worse of this by then. She knows she is not well."

Anthony drove us the 10 miles home, and we were silent except for the sobs from my sisters. They could not understand what had happened and I think they never really forgave me. My other sister Maria was at work. I had planned it deliberately because she was very sensitive and her health was delicate and I thought there was no point in her going through such trauma. But the presence of the two little ones had been vital to the plot because mother thought that with them in the car I would not do anything.

The whole experience was terrible and for years afterwards I would wake up from sleep with the same dream— that I was trapped in a room with her. Even after I was married, for several years I would wake up shouting, "No, mother, no, please, mother!"

Gradually the dreams went but the pain of that day never did. Even now I think of it with anguish. My mother did find tranquillity in the end but for the rest of her life she was in mental institutions. She lived until the age of 99, and perhaps that was fate's most cruel blow.

Now back at home with my sisters, I prepared to carry on smocking children's dresses at 20 cents each to pay the rent. Meanwhile, heavy at heart I visited Christine, who in her pregnancy showed none of the glow of the expectant mother but grew steadily weaker.

There were still several weeks to go before her baby was due, but she had to be taken in to hospital and her mother and aunt came as soon as they were notified to see her. After I had contacted them, we arranged to meet and I told them the whole story: how Christina had become pregnant by a married man, how they loved each other but she had been ashamed to tell the family, and now that she was so weak and feared she was dying, she wanted to see them.

"She was like my daughter," her aunt said. "I have no other child."

Christina's mother wept and prayed that her daughter and the baby might live, that at the hospital doctors could heal Christina's weak heart, and that a miracle could save her. I went with them to see my friend and the sight of her transparently pale skin and terrible weakness filled me with dread.

The next day Aunt Rose had to call around to the beach flat she rented out so she asked me to go to her house to cook meals for her husband, John. He was a cheerful, good-natured man and I was glad to do a good turn to Rose, who was always helping us. Marie had her day off so she was able to take care of Dolly and Marcella.

I was not there when the police car called around, and Marie said after that she had not heard the doorbell. They had come to call me to hospital, because Christina was dying.

That night I had a dream, that she was calling me. I was going down a long corridor, trying one door after another and calling her name, and she was calling, "Nan, Nan…" but I could not find her. At length I opened a door and she was here, lying still on the bed, dressed in a beautiful negligee, silent, and I felt a shiver of fear for she looked as if she was dead.

In the morning I called Anthony and asked him to drive me back to the flat, and a neighbour ran out and said, "The police were here yesterday in their red emergency car. I think your friend is very ill. They want you to go to the hospital at once."

I did, but by the time I got there, she was dead. She had had a baby girl who had also died. The loss of such a brave and loyal friend filled me with grief, like an inner void, and for a while I could think of nothing else.

Maybe it was just as well that there were soon other problems to deal with.

After the drama of getting mother to hospital, the landlord decided he had had enough of problem families. He wanted us out and the sooner the better. "By the end of the week", he said unpleasantly. In case the message had not been clearly understood, he dumped all our belongings on the pavement and locked the front door. There was no choice. We went back to Aunt Rose, who made room for us as though it were the most natural thing to do.

This, at least, would enable me to try and get a better job. Then a completely unexpected thing happened. Father turned up.

We had not seen him for a couple of years, nor had he been in contact. He had walked out as the economy crashed, borrowed money on our house, gone on the run from his creditors and when our house was repossessed by the bailiffs because of his debts and we were put out on the pavement father was over the horizon. I suspect with the rich mistress who had wanted to buy mother out. And now, here he was again.

"I want my family back," he said, embracing the little ones, "my own dear daughters. I want to look after you, to send you to school. I want you all to live with me in Ohio. And Marie,

I will send you to college to learn how to type so that you can be a secretary and earn a good living…"

Aunt Rose and I were bemused. My young sisters liked the idea of living with daddy again. For an 18-year-old I was too street-wise and cynical to take it at face value.

"So father needs to look like the responsible family man again," I thought to myself. "So he has some business deal going in Ohio and to push it through he has to act the part."

Aunt Rose and I agreed to let them go. What else could we do? I was still under age, we had no adequate means of support, and father offered a better life and security for them all.

I was sorry to see them leave; we all promised to keep in touch and the little ones declared they would write to me every week as we packed their bags and father stowed them into his car. Aunt Rose and I waved them off hoping for the best and knowing that at least it would make things much easier for us.

Lying in bed and thinking about Christina a few days later I felt into a light sleep and seemed to hear her saying, "Why don't you look after your mail, Nan? Go and pick up your mail."

Next day I went to our old flat, hammered on the front door and asked the landlord if any letters had arrived for me. "Just this," he said, thrusting an envelope into my hand and slammed the door.

I opened it and found it was a summons to an interview for the Museum Extension Project in two day's time. This was the government-sponsored job for artists to build educational models for which I had put my name down months ago. I was aghast at having nearly missed the opportunity.

I went to the interview and got the job.

I was suddenly so happy, so excited, the thought of being well paid ($150 a month ) for doing art work—the sort of work I loved and had dreamt of doing, cut through the trials and miseries of the last year and I felt that at last life was really beginning.

# Chapter 16

I started at once.

Despite the trauma of the preceding weeks I could not help feeling a leap of excitement as I took the trolley from outside Aunt Rose's house in Winton Street and travelled to the derelict factory in north Philadelphia.

It was a gaunt, square building, and its empty floors had been converted into workshops to take the fledgling Museum Extension Project and 150 new employees, of whom I was one. We were a mixed bag: from housewives with no particular skills to professional artists and sculptors who were highly skilled, carpenters, model-casters, painters, architects, black people and white—and the one thing we all had in common was the need for regular, paid work.

Our job was to design and make educational dioramas of streets, houses, interiors of historic buildings in Philadelphia and of local landscapes and wildlife, all eventually to be sent to schools and museums. This involved a lot of historical and environmental research and a variety of manual skills, and those among us who were classed as "professionals"—I was a professional painter—had to teach the others how to do it. Mr

Gotlieb's letter of recommendation had obviously counted for something, and so had all the art classes I had squeezed into the mixed bid for survival that represented my career so far.

I looked eagerly round the second floor where I was based: carpenters, labourers and model-makers round the corner, and in my area, pots of paint, Shellac and brushes and a little group mainly of women all waiting for instructions. Some were to paint landscape backgrounds for the dioramas, and others I put on room interiors, furniture and figures. My first project was a house in the middle of Philadelphia's oldest colonial street, Elfreths Alley, built near the Delaware River wharves between 1740 and 1762. The house like the rest of the alley was brick and wood. We had to paint a wooden box open fronted to show the interior, a replica of the original to the scale of half an inch to a foot, then place it within the row of house exteriors with the model street along the front lit by little gas lamps.

The interior we furnished to style like a perfect dolls' house, painted the walls, hung the curtains, and coloured the tiny figures. Time fled. Never did anyone have a more engrossed and enthusiastic workforce, and tiring though it was because the concentration was intense, it was work I enjoyed and went to happily every day.

When we had put together the house the whole model street went into a glass case made by the carpenters and it was sent round the schools. After that we painted clay models of fish found in Pennsylvanian rivers, and birds, and mounted them within painted landscapes, and did a whole Navaho Indian village with the living quarters in furnished caves to illustrate the lives of native Americans. It called for ingenuity, improvisation, perspective painting to give the impression of far distances and I was learning all the time.

A whole year passed. Not since we were torn from the refuge of grandmother's house had life been so settled. I arrived on the trolley for work at 9am with a sandwich for lunch, chatted with fellow workers over coffee in the canteen, left to go home to Aunt Rose's house in Winton Street at 5pm. or sometimes met

Anthony and his friends to go to the cinema. On summer weekends we might go to Rose's beach house in Ocean City, then on to Wildwood amusement park where we rode on the Ferris wheel and the dodgems, and danced under coloured flashing lights with the music pounding. For the first time I remember, I felt young and light-hearted. I had no particular boyfriend but not for a moment was life dull. It was a taste of normality and I relished it. Only of course there was still mother.

I did not abandon her. She had been a kind and talented mother and I loved her still and wanted her affection. The nightmare of her commitment to hospital did not disappear and though at work I could forget, every night I thought of her. The psychiatrist had said to come back in six weeks and I would find her changed, but I feared that the sight of me and the memory of how I had tricked her would make her distraught again.

When the six weeks were up, I took the train over the county border to Norristown State Hospital. Memories of the lunatic scenes in Bibury Hospital still haunted me, but here I saw only peace and quiet harmony, patients sitting in the sunshine out in the gardens, mown lawns, flowers, clean rooms and a pleasant, busy atmosphere. I walked through the park and into a sunny room.

Mother was sitting on a chair and she looked up as I entered and smiled.

I hurried to her and kissed her. She did not turn her head away. Her hair was combed, she wore a pretty dress and she said, "I'm glad to see you Nan. I've been waiting to see you and the doctor said you'd come, but I wondered…"

"You've been ill, mother," I said. "I'm so glad to see you better."

"I like it here. I've got friends."

"Theresa plays the piano for us. She's good at playing the piano," one of them said.

Mother and I spoke about my sisters, and my new job; she asked me to visit again next the next week, and would I bring her some sweets, "Oh, and some ham sandwiches…"

After that I tried to visit her every week, with her favourite sandwiches, and some money so that she could buy herself things in the hospital shop, and things to wear. "I want a dress with two pleats in front and six buttons," she said. She was very precise. "They'll give you clothes here but I don't like them." Her sense of style was still present.

I tried to get her what she wanted; the food, the clothes and she did not agitate to be discharged from the hospital. She enjoyed sewing, singing, playing the piano, sitting in the garden, but the uncertainty of mood showed itself occasionally, a reminder that out in the cold world her fragile persona could disintegrate again. Once I saved up to buy her a pretty summer dress, but it was not exactly what she wanted. "It's only got one pleat," she said angrily, "I wanted two," and she ripped it in half.

I was disappointed and annoyed. I had spent a long time choosing that dress and it was expensive. "I could have used the money," I told her. "And I brought you candy and sandwiches and you're not even pleased."

"You know what I like. Why don't you get me what I want, not rubbish," she retorted.

I picked up the dress and folded it carefully. "I'm not coming again until you write to say you want me," I said, and left. I did not go back for six weeks, then her letter came.

"I didn't mean it Nan, I was just upset that day," and when I called to see her again she was sweet and smiling and never threw a tantrum again. Indeed I would have wondered whether she could be released, but the doctor told me that she was schizophrenic with a long and difficult history and would be better off in a progressive hospital. She stayed there for 40 years, by which time Marie was married with a family and said she would take mother into her own home. The experiment did not last. In her new surroundings mother thought Marie was a stranger trying to poison her, so we found her a private rest home where she spent the remaining 15 years of her life being visited regularly.

Mother's fate is one to which I have never been reconciled but we could not change it and, still in my teens, there was the rest of life to consider. I might have closed my eyes each night with a prayer for mother, but I awoke in the mornings full of energy , optimism and enthusiasm for my work. And after a year, an added attraction appeared at the Museum Extension Project

His name was Michael and he was over six foot tall, handsome, dark, with a gentle manner, and intriguingly quiet. I thought he was shy. He spoke well, dressed well, sounded well educated and never joined in the noisy, sometimes crude bantering you get in a busy mixed workplace. He was a person apart. So what was it about him that made me feel slightly uneasy? That was simple to work out. He was attractive and deep. I wanted to make a good impression. All the girls did.

He had been taken on because he had a talent for carving and making miniature furniture including copies of Chippendale and Duncan Fyfe chairs and I was flattered when he asked me to work with him on a project to illustrate early American history. Michael Kominsky—he was the son of Ukrainian catholic immigrants—did not speak much, but he did speak to me. We had coffee together at the canteen, and discussed art. I told him about my family, my Italian background and three sisters. He told me that his father had developed cancer working in the local dye factory and went back to the farm in the Ukraine hoping to get better, leaving his wife to bring up four children, three boys and a girl on her own.

After a few weeks we started going out together in the evenings. Michael was my first real boyfriend. The French have a saying—you have to try many melons before you find a good one—but what young woman experiencing love for the first time will doubt that she is the exception? I was streetwise and naïve and I had my father's taste for romance. I dressed carefully for our evening dates: a smart suit and a pretty hat on top of my smooth, dark brown hair. I had a collection of hats and I made them all myself. Stylish, like my mother's I thought, remembering the little hats she used to perch over her lofty auburn curls.

One evening Michael took me to the Adelphi Theatre to see a musical everyone was talking about called Porgy and Bess, then on to an expensive little restaurant for supper. Afterwards we strolled across Rittenhouse Square opposite and sat on a bench in the park where, as the sky darkened, he put his arm around me and said, "Nan, I'd like to marry you, but only if you take that damned hat off." So I took it off.

It is at this point in a relationship the couple has to start meeting each other's families, an exercise which in our case was notably unsuccessful. He took me to meet his mother who had Slavic peasant features and spoke little English. She decided to impress her future Italian daughter-in-law with a big dish of spaghetti with tomato sauce and did the obvious thing—emptied two bottles of ketchup over the pasta. Michael was mortified. I tried to eat it but it was not a big success. I felt sympathetic, but our wariness was mutual. She was a short, stocky woman with careworn hands and shapeless dresses, a habit of pushing back her greying hair, and she walked in little tottering steps with her feet turned inwards. The house was in the Italian area and by this time Italians and gangsters—the name was becoming synonymous—had a shady reputation. When I had gone she told Michael that all Italians were bad people. She put it a little more graphically: "All Italians sh*t people; all your children will be crazy". Michael duly reported the conversation to me. We could have laughed, but added to Michael's reception by my side of the family it ended up serious.

We had a small engagement party with my cousin and ally Anthony and some of his friends. Everything seemed to be going quite well though the conversation was stilted at times, when Michael suddenly walked out. Had he gone to the gents? Was he ill? We speculated when he did not come back. Next day he said he had left because he did not like the music. "You've got a problem if you marry him." Anthony warned me. "He's introverted. Arrogant. Don't do it, Nan; it's a mistake."

Michael and I agreed to break the engagement but our resolve did not last long. Re-engaged, I told my friends at work and they gave me a bridal gift shower and wished me luck. But one of my work colleagues, an Italian sculptor called Millioni who was Michael's boss and who knew my family did not pretend to be pleased. I think he wanted one of his sons to marry into my family and had marked me down as a likely daughter-in-law. He was horrified to hear I was going to wed Michael. "It's a bad mistake; he'll make you unhappy," he was saying as Michael walked into the room just in time to hear.

Michael picked him up by the front of his shirt, shook him like a dog, snarled "Mind your own goddam business" and threw him back into his chair. Mr Millioni retaliated in the only way he could. He fired my husband-to-be.

That meant Michael was out of work, but we both thought he would soon get another job, and I still had mine. Our plans for the wedding went soaring ahead.

Maybe Aunt Rose wondered if she was presiding over a repeat in family history as she prepared for my wedding in mid June, but she did it with good grace and said nothing. She made me a pink suit and a little hat with flowers on it to wear at an extremely quiet ceremony in the sacristy of the church opposite grandmother's house. No one, not even my sisters, was invited : only Anthony, who gave me away, Aunt Rose and Uncle John. Michael's friend from work, a Belgian sculptor whom everyone just called Dalmassie offered us his cottage in North Wales, Pennsylvania for our honeymoon.

Uncle John was to drive us to the church but before going he had a small celebration in his office which made him very merry but not incapable of driving with extreme verve and, at times, both hands off the steering wheel.

I looked at Michael and thought how lucky I was to be marrying such a loving, and distinguished man. How handsome he looked, with his high, slightly Slavic cheekbones, clean-shaven face and dark, almost black eyes and hair. He smiled at me and said he liked my hat, and everything was about to go right forever.

After the wedding service we all went back to Aunt Rose's for the reception. Uncle John brought on his home-made wine, and Rose brought in a feast of roast lamb and salad followed by a cheesecake three inches high which was our wedding cake. Never had I been so happy. Then we, the bridal couple, left to catch the train for the 20-mile journey to North Wales, and Uncle John, slightly less capable than before, drove us to catch the train. As he took both his hands off the steering wheel to mark the beat of the song he was singing his old Buick hit two parked cars and Michael showed signs of being upset. However it all ended well and we caught the train. And when we arrived at the little wooden cottage surrounded by a grove of fruit trees, peaches and cherries ripening on the bough and flowers scattered in the grass we were enchanted with its wild prettiness.

The date was June 10th 1937, and to us everything in the world seemed perfect.

# Chapter 17

How self-absorbed lovers are, so happy with each other: we hardly noticed that the world was changing again. The threat of war was far across the ocean, in Europe, and nothing to do with us. Our world was perfect. We picked the fruit in the garden, walked across fields, learned about each other, and time drifted on for ever.

At the end of the week Dalmassie returned to his cottage but begged us to stay on. Why leave to find a flat? There was room here and no need to pay rent. So we stayed, and our payment to Dalmassie, who was a widower in his 70s and lonely, took the form of cooking meals for three and enjoying his company as we did his cottage and his garden.

Unlike Michael, the Belgian sculptor was short and wiry with sparse blond hair. We made a contented household, the three of us relaxed and easy together and the days soon fell into a pleasant pattern.

In the mornings I walked down to the railway station and took the train to the museum in north Philadelphia. It only took half an hour to cover the 18-mile journey. Sometimes Michael walked down to the station with me, then he would look for a job, which we both knew he would soon find.

I was earning good money, so there was no financial pressure. But we were children of our time, when husbands were breadwinners, and being without work made Michael feel uneasy. Getting another job was not as easy as he had expected, but he did not waste time. He took a correspondence course in precision instruments and started teaching himself mathematics, calculus and trigonometry.

Meanwhile summer drifted into autumn. Dalmassie collected baskets of plums which I made into pies, we spent long evenings with plates of pasta, drinking red wine, and Michael and I talked about the past and the future while being completely lost in the present.

He told me about his childhood living in two rooms above the poultry market in the Jewish quarter by the docks. There were four children—Michael was the eldest—three boys and a girl. Their parents were Ukrainian peasants whose new life in Philadelphia must hardly have been easier than the one they left behind. As immigrants they had arrived in the land of hope, two dots of humanity among the masses yearning to be free, and dockyard officials, unable to pronounce their foreign name casually truncated it to Kominsky, which thereafter it became.

Michael could only have been 10 years old when his father, who worked in a dye factory, became ill with cancer and abandoned his family to go back to what he thought would be the healing air of the Ukraine. Michael remembered the smell of alcohol on his breath and the scratchy moustache as his father kissed him goodbye and walked away for good. His mother Katherine spoke scarcely any English, but stayed put above the poultry mart, and scrubbed floors for a living until her hands were red and raw. She was uncommunicative, but brightened up occasionally when there was a celebration like a wedding or christening among the Ukrainian immigrants: then they would meet and dance to the balalaika and chorus the romantic, and often sad old songs that made them yearn for home.

All Katherine's children spoke Ukrainian. They seldom mixed socially with other children and Ukrainian—not even Russian—was Katherine's only language. Michael would wander around the docklands in the daytime looking for work to buy food for the family, picking up some Yiddish and English while taking in the sounds and smells of the raw immigrant area, and avoiding school.

His childhood memories cut deep. As an adult American he wrote of the constant stench of sewage bubbling into the river, "the smell of chicken-shit and empty herring barrels on the loading dock across the street," the din of porters shouting, wagons jamming the water front, black clouds of flies in the heat of summer hanging over ferry-loads of garbage going to the New Jersey pig farms. Wagon wheels and hooves squashed horse manure between the cobbles where the wind dried it and blew it into crumbling walls, seeding wild oats and grass which attracted untethered horses. Loading and unloading was reserved for black porters, who hung around in stifling heat and freezing cold in the hope of earning the price of a bowl of soup or 15 cents for half a pint of "bootleg alky".

For Michael, school was an alien place. The other children spoke English, which he did not understand, and he was an outsider with his long unkempt hair and unmatching shoes, one black and one brown, which his mother had bought for 50 cents. So he did what any sensitive boy who was a stranger outside the tribe would have done: he played truant.

The school inspectors soon had his name on their books. New age idealism had seeded a strong sense of social responsibility and the rules said all children must be educated. So the inspectors went round to the Kominsky house to rope in the truant, who always alert to capture, would climb out of a back window and run away. Eventually they called around and took all the children away, removing them from their mother's care until they had completed their education.

Michael, brought up as a Russian Orthodox, was sent to a Catholic boarding school for fatherless boys run by Jesuit brothers. Here he received a good education, learned, as far as he could, to fit into the American way of life, and acquired a thirst for reading and knowledge which never left him. So, in their respective boarding schools, did Emil, the middle brother, and Helen, their delicate and pretty little sister whom Michael adored.

His youngest brother, Johnny, was brain-damaged from the age of three after running into the path of a trolley and being hit by the push-bar. He was taught wood-working.

The Jesuit brothers found Michael a job on a farm when he left school. He was happy there, lived with the family, enjoyed the outdoor work learning about the land and looking after the animals. After six months, when it ended, he found work quarrying stone. It was heavy manual work, and sometimes dangerous, as a piece of exploding rock that cut and scarred his chin reminded him. Employment was still difficult to find when about two years later he signed on to Roosevelt's Work Progress Administration (WPA) to find a new job as I had, and was given a place on the Museum Extension Project.

As I listened to the story of Michael's childhood, the responsibility he had taken from the age of 10 for his younger brothers and sister, I could not help comparing his experiences with mine. There were so many similarities, and both of us had been rescued by good school teachers who had shown us that there was more to life than scrabbling for survival.

Maybe it was the hardships he endured and the caring for his siblings from a young age that made Michael so kind and tolerant when early in our married life we had to have my two youngest sisters to live with us.

Michael's sister had taken care of her own destiny by marrying an older man after the accidental death of a young boyfriend by drowning in the river. Now she had security, but to Michael's great distress she died young of TB. Emil became a fruit wholesaler, and had a restaurant on Front Street near the docks, and came to our rescue on many difficult occasions to come.

But for now, as we lived our idyll in Dalmassie's cottage we had no thoughts of future problems. All that seemed in the past. Michael was so clever, kind and handsome I felt that at last I had found someone to whom I could anchor my life and rely upon in any adversity.

Even happily married people say the first year of marriage is the most difficult—perhaps because when each partner thinks the other perfect, there is bound to be some disillusion. But when it happened, I was shocked.

We had been married only a couple of months when I discovered there was another side. Michael suddenly became withdrawn, as if he had cut himself off from me and he would not let me reach him. He was depressed, and isolated. Everyone likes some solitude with their thoughts, moments to themselves, but this was different. He went into his own private world, and left me.

I thought it would pass. He was, I knew, worried about not yet having a job, but that would soon change. Then one evening when I came home from work, he seemed very angry. "What's the matter?" I asked, thinking that somehow I might have offended him.

He did not reply. We ate our meal in silence, then he went to the bedroom and locked himself in. It was about 10 o'clock at night, and I was outside, pleading, "What did I do? What's the matter?"

"Just leave me alone," he shouted.

I was crying. Then it was as if the pieces of some hideous puzzle fell into place.

He was my mother.

I had seen all this before: the sudden and inexplicable anger…the withdrawal…the depression…Children repeat the problems of their parents: daughters of violent fathers marry wife-beaters; abused children abuse their own. And now, had I married a man like the mother I had taken to a mental hospital?

I had to leave.

I pushed a few things into a bag and ran down the track to the railway station. I could go to Aunt Rose…I could hardly think, I was crying so bitterly. I sat at the station, but the last train had gone. So I carried on sitting there, crying and thinking till two o'clock in the morning, then weary and cold, I walked back.

When I reached the cottage, Michael was looking out for me. "Where have you been?" he asked. "I've missed you. I've been worried…"

I looked at him with amazement. It was as if nothing had happened.

"Well you didn't have to run away," he said. "What would I have done without you? You know I love you. Look, I'm sorry. I didn't mean anything. Please stay, I want you to stay because I love you. Let's be like we were before." So I stayed. But afterwards I realised that something was not quite right.

Six months passed, and Michael still did not have a job. He was getting worried. We decided it was time to move back into Philadelphia and rent a small apartment. We found a tiny place in the north of the town. It was just one room with a communal kitchen and a shared bathroom at the end of the corridor and the room had a bed that folded back into a niche against the wall in the daytime. At night you just opened a pair of doors and pulled it down. I had never seen such a thing before, but it seemed practical and clean, and best of all, it was cheap.

Michael would be able to use it as a base for job-seeking. I was still working at the Museum Extension Project, and my sisters, to whom I wrote every week, seemed to be happily settled with father. Marie's health was still not good so father looked after her and she did not have to work, Dolly was at typing college and Marcella was still at school. It all seemed perfectly satisfactory, and our only worry was that it seemed to be much more difficult finding a job than Michael had anticipated.

The family who owned our lodging house were Italian American and as soon as we met I felt an immediate affinity with them. Michael, though, was more reserved. He was civil, but he would have preferred it if they had lived further away.

Meanwhile there was excitement in the air because the national elections were coming up; Roosevelt was running for another term and our landlord and his wife were actively canvassing on his behalf, recruiting workers and organising the local democrat campaign. They asked me if I would help. I had never thought of doing anything political before although like most people I knew, I was a big supporter of Roosevelt. I admired the way he had pulled us out of the depression and I wanted him to win. Besides, it would be fun, so I said Yes.

One of the things I had to do was to contact locally important people and ask them to attend a big social affair at Shibe Park where Roosevelt was due to appear in person to give a campaign speech. I was very excited. Michael was not. He disliked me being involved in politics, and stayed apart as much as he could while I went enthusiastically ahead.

I started to get to know a lot of people whom otherwise I would never have met. One of them was Dr. Moriarty, a wealthy man who lived in a big house down the road from us. He had two daughters with whom I became very friendly, and through them I met Grace Kelly, a pretty little girl about eight years old. The Moriartys knew her father, a handsome Irishman who had made a pile as a builder in Philadelphia but however much money he had, they still called him "that bricklayer." I expect they continued to do so even when Grace became a famous film star and married the Prince of Monaco and became Princess Grace.

At the reception I met Mrs Roosevelt, my heroine as her husband was my hero and I was proud to be working for them. I found it all exhilarating and fun, doing important work, making new friends, but Michael hated it. He was polite, but cool. He thought they were all condescending. I thought this was in his mind, that childhood feeling of being an outsider without a matching pair of shoes, which had made him stay away from school, trailing into adulthood despite all his achievements.

"We've all come from poor backgrounds," I used to tell him. "It's not what we were that matters, it's what we are now. You can be proud of the man you've become. You've got a lot to offer." I suppose being jobless didn't help, though there were many at the time in the same position.

The situation resolved itself within a few months because we decided our quarters were too cramped and moved to a new apartment in a different part of the town. This time we had two rooms and a kitchen at the top of a three-storey house in Green Street. We shared a bathroom with other tenants. It was not luxurious but we were comfortable enough.

Only a few weeks later, at the end of the day at the museum I got back home—Michael was still out looking for work—and sitting on the doorstep with their suitcases were Marie, Dolly and Marcella. Father had just brought them to our apartment and dumped them there, and they had been waiting outside all day. He had given us no warning of what he was going to do. Michael and I were stunned. The three girls were upset. All they seemed to know was, "Daddy got into some sort of trouble and he wanted to get us out of the way. He just said, 'Pack your things as fast as you can and I'll take you round to your sister's.'"

"But why?" I asked. "What did he say?"

"Some sort of trouble," Marie said. "He said he had to leave. We rang the doorbell and there was nobody in so we waited for you."

It sounded like the same old story: father getting involved in shady deals, running away from his creditors, doing another disappearing act.

"He gave us this for you," said Marcella, holding out $50.

We needed it. Michael picked up the girls' suitcases and carried them in. He was the man I had married: strong, kind, responsible. "Well, we'll start with a cup of tea," he said, and made my sisters welcome.

*My parents wedding in 1910. My father is behind his bride. On my mother's left is her eldest sister Rose, my ally in the difficult years to come, with her husband John behind her, and on my mother's right, her other sisters Josephine and Rita with their husbands.*

*Before our troubles came; me at seven years old.*

*Me with my new husband Michael Kominsky, both 21 years old on the day of our wedding, 1937. It was a small private ceremony in the church vestry.*

*Our two children Michael and Nancy.*

*My "Sunday Painters" school with students, in the sixties—Burbank, California.*

*On my way to Rome.*

*My studio/school at the YMCA in Rome.*

*Getting married to Patrick Wodehouse in 1983.*

# Chapter 18

No newly married couple, young and in love as we were, wants the family to move in with them, but somehow the five of us managed although the apartment only had two rooms. A bigger problem, and one that was starting to wear us down was that Michael had gone for nearly a year now without finding work, and he felt the stress and humiliation badly.

It was not from want of trying. It was just the times. Michael did what all the other jobless men were doing. Every day he went through the "jobs vacant" adverts. Every day he walked, to save the fare, to wherever employers were hiring men, and stood in line waiting. There were never fewer than 50 other men also waiting and sometimes over a hundred from whom one or two would be chosen. The rest walked home again to try the next day. And now suddenly we were three extra to feed and clothe.

The first thing we had to do was buy a big bed for the girls to share so we spent the $50 father had sent and they had the big bedroom while Michael and I moved to the sitting room and slept on a studio couch. It was cramped. But luckily within a week or so Marie managed to find herself a job in a nearby factory, which though it was poorly paid, helped to relieve the pressure on our budget.

Europe was moving towards war, and munitions factories were starting to take on women workers. But what was far more important as far as Marie was concerned was that she had met a good-looking Polish boy called Wallace Roginski working in the nearby steel mill. Wally was blond and charming and he had natural grace. We all liked him. They started going out together and within the year he asked her to marry him. We did not have the money to give Marie a wedding, but her future mother-in-law said that she would pay for it. So as a daughter-in-waiting Marie moved out of our rooms and into her mother-in-law's house.

Meanwhile, now that we had the other girls with us, Michael and I were looking for a little house to rent. We found a tiny one in the western suburb of Germantown—Chalmers Avenue, where the houses had been built, or, more accurately, jerrybuilt, after the war. The windows did not fit properly; there was no hot water, paint flaking off the wood... But it was bliss. It had three little bedrooms; the rent was low, only $20 a month, and it looked pretty, as rundown property often does.

The windows may have rattled and let in the draughts but they had little panes of glass that looked enchantingly old-world. There were iron railings round the front and you went up a few steps to reach the front door, which was on the side of the house with a porch over it.

We decided on sight to take it. Marie's Wally hired a horse and wagon, we piled all our belongings onto the boards, and laughing and in a thoroughly good mood we went creaking and swaying along the narrow street to our own first proper home.

It did not take long to unload our sparse belongings, carry them up the steps, through the door with its peeling paint and to set them on the living room floor.

Dolly by this time was nearly 20 years old and Marcella was 12, so they were able to help me in the house. We set about energetically making it look pretty. We rubbed down the floorboards and I painted on Shellac to varnish and seal them and it brought out the colour of the wood. Second hand furniture and walls all received their coats of paint, rich plumy pink for the main bedroom, blue and pale yellow for the other two, candlewick bedspreads and cream-coloured drapes and cushions that I ran up on an old sewing machine. Even the tiny kitchen, hardly more than a cupboard with just room for a cooking stove and an icebox looked brighter with its new ivory coloured paint and ruffled curtains.

We moved into winter and the house was warm enough so long as we kept the impressively old-fashioned black iron stove lit. It stood about five feet high on the dirt floor of the basement and we stoked it up with wood and coal, and riddled the ashes on to an open grate, in return for which it heated the radiators for the house. But there its job ended. Its remit did not run to heating water for domestic use. I had to boil that up in the kitchen, and to wash clothes I carried it in pots down wooden steps to the basement where the two washtubs stood at eye-level to the pavement. Later I used a wet-wash laundry service: linen came back damp and I dried it on the radiators.

Although there was still very little furniture the house soon started to look like the home none of us had ever had and I loved it. But contentment was mingled with unease.

The stress of Michael not having a job was beginning to make him morose, with periods of depression, which the rest of us did not know how to handle. He would ignore the two girls and sometimes go for a few days hardly speaking to me. His moods imposed a threatening heaviness over the household, like a cloud, and although the girls and I carried on as if nothing was happening, the atmosphere was anything but relaxing. I still had my job at the museum, which I enjoyed, for the work was pleasant and sociable and the money held us together, but my $140 a month was having to go a long way.

Dolly was never a career girl. She liked family life and she knew just what she wanted: a husband and children. While she waited she found a job in a fast-food chain called Bob's

Hamburgers, which meant she was able to pay something for her keep. She was by now a vivacious, pretty girl, with dark curly hair and dark eyes, and she was looking out for a suitable young man to marry. As luck would have it the nearest available unattached man was William Geiger who lived next door and I did not think he was at all suitable. He was 23 years old, of German extraction like most of our neighbours, thin, unattractive and dull. He had been discharged from the Army on health grounds. Nobody liked him very much but Dolly insisted he had hidden depths, which apparently only she could see, and in the end she did marry him. They eloped to Maryland and had a child called Billy but it only lasted for a year.

In the meantime we lived together just about managing on my salary. The girls had to be clothed as well as fed, and we had not forgotten about mother. I visited her every week, as I had since she was committed to hospital. It involved taking two buses and a train each way because she lived in a different suburb so it took a lot of time but it was worth it for our peace of mind and because she was always glad to see me.

Before going I would make some of her favourite ham sandwiches and often things for her to wear. Her face would light up as I entered her room, but she was still withdrawn. When the weather was good we could go out into the grounds and sit on the park benches, a source of enjoyment to us all because the lawns and flowerbeds were well kept and there was a fine variety of trees. The hospital staff told me that on her good days mother would play the piano for them and because she was such a good seamstress she was in much demand to help with the sewing.

She looked tidy and clean, though without her old elegance. I saw in her face a kind of resignation, almost contentment, and certainly more peace than she had felt during the ravaged years when she felt the world plotting against her. Even so, almost every time I visited she asked me when I was going to take her home. I discussed it with the doctor, and he said that she would never be mentally fit enough to leave, so I was vague with my answers, and said I was speaking about it to the medical supervisor. I always felt a shadow of sadness as I said this, remembering the affectionate and capable mother she had been and as I went home I often thought of the days when I watched her dress her hair with all the admiration of a little girl for a pretty mother and she made me feel grown-up by treating me as her confidante. When I took my sisters to see her we would sit in the garden with her and I glossed over the future, just telling them that she was not yet quite better yet but was well looked after.

For several months we lived like a family in our small house. Then I lost my job. It was devastating.

The Museum Extension Project closed because Roosevelt's emergency work programmes were coming to an end. Officially the Depression was over. But it was not over for everyone.

Industry was picking up, galvanised by the war in Europe although most Americans were determined to stay out of it, but men were still scouring the adverts and queuing to be hired.

Michael and I were desperate. Now I was on the same trek as he: going through the adverts, walking the streets applying for jobs. We lived on vegetables and rice and the cheapest food I could get together.

Eventually I saw an advert for Gimbles' store where they were hiring women for an in-store boutique called Jane Engle. I decided I must get it. At that time fashion magazines were very dictatorial about how smart women should dress and in Pennsylvania we took a lot of notice of things like that. The smart lady's uniform was a little black dress for every occasion, and for stepping out into the street, even if only to do some quick shopping, she should always put on white gloves and a hat. So when I applied for the job at Gimbles' new boutique, I followed the rules.

From my two dresses, I picked the black one and lightened the neckline with a double string of pearls. I put a little hat on my dark, elegantly-chignoned hair and drew on the white gloves. It did not hurt that I had a good figure. Then I went early and stood in the line.

Everyone seemed to be trying to get this job. I was the only one dressed up as for a catwalk and after what Michael had told me about standing and waiting endlessly to be hired I felt pretty upset. Only days before he had applied to be taken on to learn the refrigeration business—at just $5 a week—and been turned down even for that. I could see ahead another week, and another, of eating carrots and rice and worrying about the future.

As I stood there dumbly waiting, a man came out of the office. He was Mr Kaufmann who was married to Gimbels' daughter. He saw me—I stood out from the others because of my clothes and height—and said, "Would you like to be a mannequin?"

We call them models now. Would I like to be a model? Wouldn't I just! I said. "I'm waiting for a job."

Come into my office," he said. I followed him in. "This is a very select shop," he said. "I think you'd do well as a mannequin." The money was not very good but it was enough to keep us going for now. And not only was the job fun and sociable, there were also perks.

One was that as an employee I could get 25% off the price of furniture and other goods at the store. And I could buy things on hire-purchase. The instalment plan was a new idea introduced during the depression to reduce stock, which could not be shifted when people had no ready money to put down the full price at once. Mr Kaufmann used to say that the hire purchase scheme and Roosevelt had saved their bacon and kept retailers in business. When he knew that I had met Mrs Roosevelt he used to come to speak to me often.

There were two other models working with me, both tall, elegant girls from socially prominent families. They were there, they said, "for a lark"—not really in need of the money—but they were friendly and we got along well together. Through them I met many people, some of whom I knew already from when I was helping to canvass for Roosevelt: Dr Mitchell, whose daughter, Alice was one of the models, the Morriartys , the Kellys, whose daughter Grace was now nearly a teenager…But the greatest bit of luck at this time was that Michael found a job. And it was a good, well-paid, secure job.

After being one of more than a hundred men standing in a line for the $5 a week refrigeration job and not being taken on, Michael went to the terminal in Reading to shelter from the rain and he found $5 lying on the ground. He decided to buy a cup of coffee. While he was there, he bumped into an old friend, Frank Ray, whom he had met and liked when we were staying with Dalmassie in North Wales. Michael as a rule was so unsociable he never liked guests, but Frank and his wife had called round for supper several times and the two men had got on well together. Michael had been studying precision instruments, calculus and trigonometry and had a natural bent for detailed and precise work which Ray admired.

"What are you doing now?" Frank asked.

Michael confessed that he was desperate for work. I was not earning much. The two girls were with us. He had been jobless for a year…

Frank was aghast. He worked for the Brown Instrument Company where they made precision equipment for submarines, and with the prospect of war drawing nearer they had just taken a big order from the government. Men with Michael's qualification were like gold dust. "Come and see me in North Wales," he said. Michael was there next day and he was taken on at a good salary. When later he tried to leave during the war to join the Army he was refused permission because his work was considered vital and he stayed on for the duration.

About six months into my modelling job at the boutique I became pregnant. Michael was not pleased. "There's too much trouble in the world to bring in children," he said—but what could we do? Anyway, I wanted children. I told Mr Kaufmann who said I could keep my job because part of it was in the sales department and we models each had our own mailing lists of clients. So I carried on working until the last three weeks, and then went back a few months after the birth.

During that time I was able to transform the house, thanks to the reduced prices and 25% concession for staff at Gimbals and the instalment payment scheme.

The living room had had hardly any furniture. Now I bought a beautiful mahogany Governor Winthrop desk with a mahogany desk-chair; a wing chair upholstered in pale blue silk, a love-seat covered in rose silk with little roses embroidered on it, a side table and an elegantly-carved mirror. The cushions were stuffed with the softest down and covered in silk. And the drapes were in shades of blue and plum with a small colonial print, falling from a valance against the deep-set windows. The room looked beautiful. Two expensive Aubusson rugs made it complete.

In the dining room we had an early American style table and six chairs. Michael was very good at re-doing furniture and now he designed a dresser, which an Italian carpenter made for us, and he stained it with tung-oil till it had a deep, honey-coloured patina. On it I displayed the willow-pattern china my friends at the museum had given me as an engagement present. Michael's brother Emil gave us a fine cedar chest on legs, which we could use to store linen, and as a table. And ready for the baby I put a crib in the small bedroom and a little chest of drawers and wardrobe. Now I knew how my mother must have felt when we were in Hicks Street and father indulged her sense of style and love for pretty things and the pleasure she took in arranging them about the house.

When the time came I went to hospital, and in August of 1940 my daughter Nancy was born. She had golden brown curls and brown eyes and was strong, healthy and beautiful, everything I had hoped for. My youngest sister Marcella was now 15 years old and a willing helper and baby-sitter when I went home. After I went back to work at Gimbels', she stayed at home to look after Nancy full-time and I paid her a few dollars a week from my earnings.

So for the moment the scene seemed set for perfect happiness: a baby, two weddings, a doting young aunt who enjoyed baby-minding, and a comfortable home. Michael went every day to do a job he found interesting and which used his talents to the full, and we had security. And yet ... something was out of joint.

Michael loved his little daughter. Though he had not wanted a child, now he was enchanted by her pretty ways. But there was something else that I did not understand: his moods, the sudden explosions of anger, the periods of depression and silence, the refusal to have anything to do with normal social life and anger when I did. Interspersed were his expressions of love, passionate declarations that he could not live without me, pleading his need for me that pulled at my heart. What was it about? Maybe I was at fault. Maybe it would come right. Maybe—I pushed away the thought—I had made a mistake.

# Chapter 19

This was a strange time to be living in Germantown because the war against Nazi Germany cast its shadow from Europe across the Atlantic and national feelings were reflected among the new immigrants of America.

When we went out into the streets of Germantown we heard German spoken: food shops were stocked with bratwurst, weisswurst, sauerkraut, dark rye bread, flavours to remind the new Americans of the homes they had left behind in a country now at war and against which President Roosevelt seemed to be showing unashamed prejudice.

Our neighbours on both sides were German—the Geigers, whose son was briefly married to Dolly, and on the other side, an elderly couple, Mr and Mrs Baumann, who had always been friendly and kind to me. We got on well together. But Mr Baumann had a small arms factory, and everyone around knew he wanted Germany to win the war and was exporting machinery from his firm to the Fatherland.

At this time we all listened avidly to the radio news, tension and intolerance rising with the fear of conflict. There was local backbiting. The Baumanns and their friends belonged to a

German association working actively for the Nazis and naturally they did not like Roosevelt nor his Anglo Saxon sympathies. They referred to him contemptuously as "the cripple", which of course he was. To me, Roosevelt was a hero, our saviour in the Depression. He promised to keep us out of the war, but we knew that if neutrality failed we would be on the Allies' side.

A certain coolness developed between the Baumanns and me. Of course in times like these one should never have mentioned politics to neighbours from such diverse backgrounds, but the war became the backdrop to all our other activities. And those were difficult enough.

While Marcella looked after Nancy in the daytime I was able to continue working at Gimbles. Michael had become an important member of the Brown Instruments Company where they made equipment for submarines, travelling to North Wales every day and returning tired in the evenings, often with more studying to do at night to keep up with developments. My main worry was that if war broke out he would probably be conscripted, or more likely, he'd volunteer and go to Europe. Then suddenly we had something else to worry about.

Marcella had gone out for the evening with some of her teenage friends and was brought back a few hours later by the police who said they caught her joyriding in a stolen car and she would have to go to court, Michael was furious. I was dismayed. And Marcella was in tears, denying that she knew anything about the car being stolen and thought it belonged to one of her friend's parents.

Michael had to take a day off from work to go to court and sort it out. One of the teenagers in the dock backed Marcella's story and she was released, but Michael was still angry with her and decided she needed proper supervision and discipline. So we agreed that Marcella should go back to High School—she was barely 16 years old—where she could finish her education and learn to type. I gave up my job in Gimbles and stayed at home to look after Nancy.

The house was so pretty and my little daughter so lively and enchanting I settled easily into the domestic life. Marcella would come back after school and sometimes take the baby out for a walk while I cooked the evening meal—but she never chatted or confided in me as one might have expected of a younger sister. She was tall, shapely, pretty with chestnut curls, but quarrelsome and withdrawn. She liked to go to her own room and write poetry. Perhaps she was just being a typical adolescent. None of us had been able to afford adolescence. But Marcella, more than Maria, Dolly or I, had suffered from the lack of family background. She had never known a mother who was not mentally distraught and unhappy, or a father who acted like one. All her life had been insecure and a struggle against poverty, the little girl towed along in the wake of events she could neither understand nor control. And because she was the baby of the family I do not think the rest of us realised that she was suffering as well.

At this time there were other things to occupy us. Some of my friends commissioned me to paint their portraits, and I painted flowers on plates and tea-trays and sold them to a gift shop down the road while Nancy played with the little boy of my next-door-but-one neighbour, an English woman called Ruth Minick. Life seemed settled, but of course it never is.

Without warning one day, Marcella packed her bags and left. She had met an older man. Exactly how old he was I do not know because we never met: Marcella had not even mentioned him, but she married him in Philadelphia without telling us, and they lived in the same town though we did not know where. She did not contact me again for a few years. I supposed she wanted to make her own decisions but I felt hurt because we had been a close family and had gone through many things together.

Now my three sisters were all married but for a long time none of them kept in touch. Neither Dolly's nor Marcella's marriage lasted more than one year. Marcella married again, almost as briefly, a young student, and finally met John Lynn with whom she had two sons and a daughter.

Despite missing my sisters, events moved forward swiftly and there was no time to dwell on the past. Nationally there was a feeling of impending disaster but when it came it was sudden and completely unexpected. I remember the shock as radio bulletins gave the news. It was Sunday, December 7 in 1941 and many of the shop windows had already been dressed for Christmas when the astounding announcement came that the Japanese had bombed Pearl Harbour. We called the Japanese the "Yellow Peril" but we had been fed on propaganda: they all had terrible eyesight; their weapons were badly-made and out of date... Now we saw the reality as the horror of the attack was revealed. In two hours 19 of our warships had been sunk, 188 aircraft destroyed on the ground and as a result 2,403 of our service men and women lost their lives. We were aghast at the unannounced treachery. With eyesight and weaponry as good as ours, the Japanese had sent over more than 300 bombers and fighter aircraft in a pre-emptive strike, having already signed a pact with Germany. There was only one answer. War. President Roosevelt made the announcement on the radio. My heart sank. We all knew that this was not going to be a short war but heaven only knew what losses it would bring.

Even as Michael and I settled into family life, the nearest to normal domesticity either of us had experienced, with our daughter and comfortable home, the stresses that would disrupt it were already there.

First came a heartbreaking family tragedy that drove Michael further into the depression and mental isolation that never entirely left him. His loved young sister, Helen, who was only in her twenties had tuberculosis, the killer disease of the period. Michael's spurts of anger and periods of silent despair had never included tears, but now he sobbed broken-heartedly. In the last day of her illness he stayed by her bedside until she died and afterwards shut himself up in his room and cried and cried, rejecting comfort and the rest of the world and finding refuge only in sleep. When he had problems he often used to go to bed and sleep but this was the first time I had seen him so emotionally broken and I felt the desolation of being shut out. His withdrawal and coldness had become a feature of our marriage yet there were times when he was loving and we were happy.

Helen had had a little daughter now two years old, the same age as Nancy and after her mother's death she came to live with us. She stayed for a year and the girls played happily together, Nancy robust, blonde and healthy and her cousin with her mother's delicate looks and Irish father's dark curly hair. I bought them pretty dresses and pinafores and took them for walks and they were a joy to us both.

Michael loved the two little girls and they adored him, waiting for him to come home after work and greeting him with giggles and kisses and demands to be picked up. He was a good and kind father. And he was working hard and earning enough for me to make a proper home for us all without worrying about money. So I painted and cooked and stretched our wartime rations of meat and sugar, which Michael's younger brother Emil who was shorter and less attractive-looking than he but more practical and easy-going, would augment with presents of tuna fish in tins and other treats he was able to get because he worked in the docks.

I was always glad to see Emil, not because of the gifts he brought, but because he was as cheerful and friendly as Michael was the opposite. Later he opened a restaurant near the docks and was married and had a daughter called Ellen whom he adored.

By this time I realised that Michael was not the man I thought I had married. What I had seen as attractive shyness I now saw as arrogance, his silences as indifference to other people. He was a loner who disliked people and I was gregarious with lots of friends.

My friends were not welcome in his house. If they came to tea I ushered them out before Michael came home from work. As he now often worked late this was not difficult but I wanted some social family life and one day asked a couple to dinner.

Michael pointedly ignored them, did not bother to reply when they spoke to him, then to our embarrassment got up from the table, lay down on the sofa and went to sleep. I tried to make excuses; they said they understood, hard work and all that, and left in a hurry. I was mortified and angry but Michael shrugged and said they were stupid people anyway and he was going to bed.

I trod carefully, cooking, looking after the children, visiting mother at the hospital, cleaning the house, making sure friends and strangers were out of the way by the evening. By this time most young men of draft age were in uniform and Michael wanted to join up as well. He had tried once and been turned down on the grounds that the work he was doing was essential to the war effort but now, in 1943 he was starting to feel unpleasantly conspicuous in civilian clothes. Then in the spring of 1943, I became pregnant again. I was delighted. Michael was not.

He was furious. "This is a terrible world," he shouted. "You shouldn't bring any more children into it. It's irresponsible! There's a war on! Why do we need more children?"

"I didn't have this child alone," I retorted but he was not listening.

"Well don't bother me with it," he said angrily. He was tired and upset about work conditions and doing long hours. He wanted to enlist because he said that when the war was over he could have problems if he did not get into the fight but they would not let him because he was not allowed to leave his work on submarine instruments.

He was tall, physically fit and draft-age and strangers on the street seeing us together would jeer, "That's right, get her pregnant then you don't have to go", because at that time they were not taking men with a first child. Sometimes he had to get off the train to avoid trouble and there were occasions when I had to drag him away to stop him getting into a fight. In the end he told the instruments company that if they would not release him he would quit. "We don't have time to train anybody else to your level," they protested. But Michael had had enough. He handed in his notice, walked out and stayed at home for a week. It was no good: they sent the police around to get him back. His brother joined the Navy as a cook. Michael was grounded at home.

His anger was always close to the surface and now his frustration at being out of uniform made him kick against the gourds of domesticity. He wanted nothing to do with a new baby.

My cousin Anthony's wife came to see me with her child. They had whooping cough but, she assured me, her doctor had told her she was past the infectious stage so we would be all right. But we were not. Nancy and I both caught it and we were both very ill. Between nursing Nancy I was so sick I could hardly stand. Despite our political differences my German neighbours were kind and helped me where they could and when Nancy was over the whooping cough Ruth would take her in to play with her own little boy.

It took me longer to get better and then I was weak. The doctor said I was anaemic and should eat more meat, but as it was rationed this was not easy. Eggs were not on ration at that time, and Emil used to bring some fish—and sometimes I also had some extra pieces of meat from German Jewish immigrants, the Rosenbergs who owned the kosher meat mart in Germantown.

The year wore on to December when the baby was due and still Michael was working long hours and took little interest. The shops were gearing up for Christmas, a more austere one than usual because of the war, but some coloured lights were twinkling when I started to have labour pains. Friends took me to Lankenau Hospital, and then, when the pains subsided and nothing happened, home again. The pains started again and I went back to hospital, and this time because transport was a problem they decided to keep me there and induce the birth.

The hospital was crowded with women having babies. It seems to be one of the things that happens in wartime: in the face of possible death and the destruction of the social order, young men and women have babies. There were women giving birth in the corridors, women on stretchers, apparent confusion... My baby's birth was not easy. Nurses hurried to get the duty intern from a Christmas party and he delivered my son with forceps.

As I held the long, skinny baby in my arms I felt love mingled with exhaustion and a touch of anxiety because one of his eyes was closed. The doctor said he would be all right and went back to the Christmas party. And next day I had to go home to make room for the next patient. "I'm sorry, we need the bed," the nurse told me apologetically as she swaddled the crying baby. I rang Michael at work and asked him to come and take me home but he was irritable and said he was too busy. Upset and feeling unwell I rang his brother Emil who came at once. He was shocked, partly because I was being sent home while still so weak and because Michael had refused to help. "He's a problem," Emil said. "I don't know what's the matter with him."

My friend Ruth Minick said she would look after Nancy until I could manage and it was a relief knowing that my daughter was happy with her little boy and being well cared for just two doors away from me. I was able to concentrate on the new baby.

It was mid winter, the house was freezing because coal was rationed and we could not get any. The neighbours tried to get a special pass for us so that I could buy some but they failed, so I wrapped the baby in outdoor clothes, wore a coat myself and lit the kitchen oven to give some warmth. It was a bleak Christmas. But I felt the happiness of a mother with the miracle of a new-born baby. And I also felt fear for the future that had become so uncertain.

# Chapter 20

W e called the baby Michael, like my husband.

   Despite problems at birth, I expected the new baby to thrive, soon to put on weight and take notice of the world he had just entered, as Nancy had. But he did not. His right eye remained closed. A septic discharge came from it and although I bathed it several times a day it seemed to make no difference. He cried all the time.

   The house was cold and I kept him well wrapped up but the eye remained closed and he kept on crying until I felt like crying myself with exhaustion. I rang Aunt Rose.

   Comforting like a mother she told me to take Michael straight away to the eye hospital in Philadelphia where a doctor examined him and said it had been injured by forceps during the birth. "The eye is so badly infected, if it doesn't clear up in a week we might have to remove it," the doctor said. I was horrified. He gave me ointment to put on it and I left the hospital with Michael wrapped up in a shawl, full of fear.

   My husband was working long hours and although he was concerned for his son, he could not handle pressure and told me I would have to deal with the problem myself. So I prayed. All my life I have prayed about things I could not handle alone and now for nine days I implored God to save the baby's eye and make him better.

On the ninth day Michael's right eye opened just a little, and the discharge stopped. I took him back to the hospital and the doctor said, "We seem to have a miracle here. It looks as if he's responding to treatment." By the end of the next two weeks the eye had opened completely.

All this time Ruth had carried on looking after Nancy for me. Now at last I could have my daughter back but it was not for long. The baby suddenly developed a very high temperature and seemed to be struggling to breathe. Ruth took Nancy again and I took a taxi to the hospital with Michael where the doctors thought his symptoms looked like pneumonia. But it wasn't. They tested him for meningitis and it was not that either. He seemed to get better and I took him home again. This was a pattern that repeated itself for the next two years.

Numerous times I thought we were going to lose him; he was thin and fretful and had feverish attacks when his breathing became laboured. As he lay one day on his hospital bed he slipped into a coma, his colour changed and I knew he was dying. I called the nurses who rushed to bathe him in iced water, which brought his temperature down, and he regained consciousness. But there seemed no cure. Antibiotics made no difference. In the end the doctors told me that they gave little chance for his survival unless we took him to live in a warm climate.

I told my husband and we both decided we should give up the house at once: sell the furniture, and I should go as soon as possible to California with the baby.

Aunt Rose's husband had a married niece called Marie who lived in California. Marie said I could stay with them in Beverley Hills, "but don't bring children or animals," she warned. "California's a boom town: everybody wants to live here and you can't find accommodation. Houses are terribly expensive and nobody renting out rooms will take children."

With that warning in mind we decided that Nancy should stay in Philadelphia and board at a convent school recommended by a friend who knew one of the nuns. My husband could not leave his work so he rented rooms in North Wales and saw Nancy every week.

It was 1945 and although the war in Europe had ended, we were still fighting the Japanese. The train was crowded and the journey took three days and nights, the temperature rising and the skies turning blue as we rattled down south to California. When I stepped off the train carrying Michael, warm, scented air embraced us, and there was Marie, arms outstretched, beaming smiles and welcome.

Marie was short and slight of build but she had a big, warm personality. She was married to a restaurant owner, Tony Bianca who was just a bit taller than herself and considerably rounder. He was always laughing and joking, and they had a little dog, which liked to have ice cubes in his water. They were delighted to add a real baby to the household and insisted on charging no rent.

Michael had been unwell on the journey and cried all day and the next. The feverish attacks and breathing difficulties continued: many nights he woke up and cried and because the house was small he must have disturbed Marie and Tony. Neither ever complained but I felt I was imposing upon them because they both worked day and night shifts at the restaurant and needed to sleep.

I started to look around for rooms to rent.

Housing was at such a premium in California at this time, it seemed that anyone with a modest garden-size patch of land was sitting on a fortune. Developers were moving in and they couldn't build fast enough. Aircraft manufacturers like Boeing and Lockheed were in the area working at full production, employing thousands of women as well as men on war work so there was also a demand for children's nurseries. It was like a frontier town, money being made fast and spent just as quickly.

I found a room. Two sisters, both widows in their sixties who shared a charming old house with big rooms were renting one with use of kitchen and small bathroom for $100 a month. I did not tell them I had Michael when I took it, and when they saw him; they said I could keep him until I found a nursery. I found one in Glendale, near my room, run by a woman who seemed efficient, though I did not much like her. I asked her about medical care and she said, "Oh yes, we have all sorts of professional help here." The furniture looked good. And the fee was high—$100 a week. I reluctantly booked Michael in, consoling myself that I could visit him every day.

Now I had to get a job. I scoured the newspaper adverts and found one, painting Dresden figures at a factory. I enjoyed the work; it was artistic and the people I worked with were friendly, but it only paid $42 a week. Although my husband sent me a small sum of money every week , I had to earn more, so I turned to the newspaper ads again.

With so many people on war work there was a shortage of labour and I quickly found the Rancho Restaurant where they were so desperate for help they were hiring waitresses without bothering about experience.

It was a beautiful restaurant, with low, beamed ceilings, booths for the tables and French windows leading to a pretty garden. It was always full. I went for an interview and the manageress did not bother to ask me if I had ever worked in catering, she just said, "What size uniform do you need? You'll do. Start tonight." So that evening I donned a green cotton dress with a white pinafore and white frilly cap, and started work.

It was a madhouse, but a cheerful one, and the staff all looked out for each other. I soon learned to carry five plates along my arm, and to dodge people and tables with a tray piled with six main-course meals. The old hands—the hashers, we called them—passed on some of the tricks of the trade. One of them, Marion, had bright red hair which she dyed herself and she used to drive to work in a big car and prime herself with a couple of stiff martinis before getting down to earning big tips.

Early on she initiated me in the ways of augmenting my measly wage of 75 cents an hour. "This is how it's done," she said, with a big wink. "Watch me." She flipped open a napkin and laid it on a lady's knees, then did the same for the husband, just touching his legs as she did so. "Always works," she said.

The Rancho was not far from Lockheed Aircraft and during lunchtimes it was packed with people who worked there. In the evenings, families came in because food was rationed, and on Sundays they brought all their children. I was soon earning $100 a week in tips alone and managing to pay for my room and Michael's nursery. But I was not happy with the nursery. I called in one day and found that five babies were all sharing a bedroom hardly bigger than a cupboard. One of the waitresses at the restaurant came to my aid: she said she knew a married nurse in her early forties who was childless but longed to have babies and she would love to look after Michael. That was how I met Frances.

Frances was a find. She had short, dark hair, a slim figure and a husband who worked at Lockheed, but what endeared her to me and eventually to Michael, Nancy and my husband, was that she had lots of common sense and she loved the children.

She treated Michael's breathing and mucus problem like a bad cold, dosed him with cough syrup and aspirin and kept him warm. In the summer she took him to the beach and encouraged him to swim and exercise. He learned to walk without falling over at last; she gave him good food and he started to put on weight and to grow. But he was still thin and when he wore saddle shoes—he had big feet—he reminded me of Mickey Mouse.

I worked lunches at the restaurant, and then had from 3 to 5pm off before starting work for the evening, so every afternoon I was able to see them both. Michael was now three years old and seemed to be getting better. He was still having feverish attacks with breathing difficulties but now he had one every few weeks, whereas before it had been at least once a week. The cause remained a mystery. He was eight years old before he was completely better.

With the war in Europe at an end, my husband was writing to us saying how much he missed us and now at last he thought he could give up his job in North Wales and come down with Nancy to join us. The aircraft manufacturers in California were still taking in specialist staff for the Japanese war and I was sure that with my husband's qualifications he would soon get work. I longed to see my six-year-old daughter again.

One problem was that I was still living in one room. The only way we could manage was for Nancy to join her three-year-old brother with Frances, who said she could easily look after them both, and my husband shared my rented room. It had to be a temporary solution because we were too cramped, and once again one of the waitresses at the Rancho Restaurant came to my aid. She knew of a couple that were splitting up. They wanted to sell their house, but meanwhile they would be glad to let us live in it at a low rent rather than leaving it empty.

We moved in. It was a beautiful building with good furniture, a front porch and a big garden full of roses and vines and a magnificent collection of brilliantly coloured dahlias. For six months we were there while looking for something more permanent.

Eventually through an agency we found a run-down house in a suburb, Sun Valley for rent and we paid $500 to move in. It was badly in need of a lick of paint and repairs but my husband was good at that. He worked hard day after day. We found second hand furniture and I went to the department store nearby and bought bed linen and china on the never-never. At last Nancy and Michael were able to join us and I gave up my job at the restaurant to look after them.

To help pay the rent we let out one of the bedrooms to a Rancho waitress whose husband was still away with the Army. My husband found a job working on precision tools at the aircraft company belonging to the eccentric multi millionaire Howard Hughes so we were financially secure, but we could do with some extra money because there were so many things we needed to buy for the house. I looked around for some work I could do at home and found it at a nearby ceramics factory where they produced candy boxes decorated with painted ceramic roses. My job was to make the roses. They supplied the clay and boxes, I shaped the three-inch flowers, packed them in rows and sent them back to be fired and painted. Soon I was earning as much as I had at the restaurant.

When September came Nancy started school in the first grade. The school bus picked her up from the corner of the block every day and brought her back in the afternoons. She began to find new friends, and Michael's attacks were becoming more spaced-out. My husband took an interest in both the children. He helped them with their schoolwork and a bond of affection grew between them.

My sister Dolly, divorced from her first husband was now also living in California not far from us with her little boy, Billy, who was about eight years old. She needed to find a full-time job, which was difficult as a single mother, so she asked me if we would take Billy into our family for a while. It was a happy arrangement for us all and he stayed about two years. My husband's own difficult childhood made him sensitive to Billy's need for security and he welcomed the little boy like another son. Billy responded by loving his uncle.

At the weekends my husband would take the three children down to the beach and I would follow on with the picnic. I still remember with longing the sunshine glittering on the warm sea, the children playing with their father on the sand, a cameo of the happy family life that might have been ours...

We were not worried about money. We were even able to save a bit to buy a house of our own one day and anyone glancing in at our domestic life might have thought it a scene of familial contentment. But it was not.

My husband hated his job at the aircraft factory and became increasingly morose and angry. Anything could spark his rage. One of the things that did was the sight of my work, my clay roses in boxes waiting to be sent to the kiln. "Can't you get rid of that junk?" he'd shout at me. I couldn't.

None of my friends were allowed to cross the threshold and I tried to snatch social moments when Michael was at work but there was constant stress. One day Marie and Tony who had helped me so generously when I first arrived in California called around to see us. It should have been a happy reunion and I wanted to show them my appreciation by making a special dinner for us all. But my husband reduced it to pure embarrassment. He pointedly would not speak to them. He flung himself onto the sofa and pretended to sleep. I was in tears. After Marie and Tony left he shouted, "Why do they have to come here? I don't want to see them again!" and he stormed out of the house.

I no longer dared to invited friends to our house: it would only provoke a row. My husband was morose and could be silent for days. His depression seemed to have no recognisable trigger. There were good times: when we were alone he could be loving and then I would remember why I had married him. But there was always an undercurrent of anger, the threat of an explosion, which kept us in a perpetual state of unease.

Even when my husband's dream of buying our own house materialised, peace of mind eluded him and we all lived in fear of his outbursts.

The house was a bungalow, part of a small estate built in an olive grove in Burbank, and it was being sold off cheaply because the builder had gone bankrupt. We applied, borrowed some of the $500 deposit money, managed to get a low-interest mortgage and became owners of a pretty home with three bedrooms and a 75-metre garden containing six olive trees. The other bungalows were built at different angles in the grove to look like a little village. The kitchen had modern fittings; the sitting room was spacious with a fireplace in the corner and three big doors led to the garden. Casement windows with small panes gave the place a cottagey look. We all loved it. Even my husband seemed happy there. He was proud of owning his own house in a good neighbourhood; he painted it, made a patio, and I planted flowers in the garden.

The children both settled into school, took part in local events, had friends, Michael became good at swimming and basketball... But my husband could never be at peace for long. He wrote to his brother that he did not like living in California: he missed Philadelphia. He wanted to go back. And that's what he did.

Emil came to visit us in California and despite my obvious reluctance he went along with my husband's decision to quit living down south and go back to Pennsylvania right away. Emil had reason to agree: he was divorced from his wife and had his teenage daughter Elena living with him. Nancy would be a good companion for Elena He had a restaurant to run and my husband could do the books. So he spent his own money buying a house for us in Philadelphia, a new one with woodland and a stream at the back and it was all arranged: my husband and Nancy should go back with him and I should sell our bungalow in the olive grove, pack up our furniture, and follow on with Michael.

It seemed that our life under the Californian sun had come to an abrupt end. I sold the house, packed our bags and caught the train with Michael for the three-day journey north. I knew by now that my husband was not going to be happy anywhere, but even I could not have guessed that within four months I would be taking the train back once again to California.

# Chapter 21

The house Emil bought us in Philadelphia was part of a new estate in a park and it was almost like living in the country again. Although I had not wanted to leave California, I thought that now our son's health was better we could be happy living here, but we did not have a chance to try. Before we even unpacked all the furniture my husband started to wish he hadn't come back to Pennsylvania after all.

He was on edge and moody. His over-dependence on Emil made him angry and I could see his frustration growing. He was working at Emil's restaurant doing the books; Emil paid him, and we lived in the house Emil had bought us. Emil, well meaning as he was, should have known from experience that his brother would become quarrelsome, angry, and impossible to work with.

"Let's go out for a drive," Michael said to me one evening. "We've got ourselves into a fix. We've got to talk about it. You'll have to go back, get a house and a job in California, get the children back to school…"

"But the furniture has only just arrived," I protested—and so had the organ a friend had given me for painting her portrait and my collection of old bottles.

"Why did you bring those damn bottles with you? Michael exploded. "Haven't we got enough rubbish to cart around already?" He was in one of his sudden furies.

"They're antiques…" I started to cry as he swerved angrily down streets in a part of the town I did not know. Suddenly he leaned over, opened the car door and shoved me out while the vehicle was still moving and sped on leaving me sprawled on the road. It was getting late. I got up and wiped my grazed knees and walked slowly to a drugstore, which still had a light on inside. It was open, and I telephoned Emil. He came at once, full of concern, helped me into his car and as he drove me to Aunt Rose's house, he said, "I don't know what's the matter with my brother. I thought I was doing you a favour, buying that house… if you want to go back to California, I'll pay your fare."

I did not have much choice. Emil said he would send us some money. My sister Dolly had married again and still lived in California with her son Billy and her new husband. She said we could stay with them until they helped us find somewhere else to live. So my husband remained in Philadelphia while Nancy and Michael and I packed a suitcase each and made the three-day train journey back to California.

This time there was no sense of adventure. I was glad to see Dolly again, pretty as ever with her dark curly hair and shining blue eyes, now happily married to Bob Crowe, whom we all liked. He was a large man, with a big sense of humour, sandy hair, blue eyes, and we laughed when we heard he was the cook in the local prison. As we soon found, he was a good cook, too. He loved children although he had none of his own, and he was a loving stepfather to Billy. His welcome to us was as warm as Dolly's.

We went to their house in the San Fernando Valley. Though cramped it was a relief to be away from my husband's volcanic moods. Within a month Dolly heard of a family nearby who were going to Japan for a year and wanted to let their half-furnished house for $75 a month. It was in a good area, and I took it.

Nearby a doctor was up-dating his furniture to pine and selling off some beautiful old pieces, which I bought. My brother-in-law sent us money regularly for basic needs and soon our home was comfortable and pretty. The children went to school and I went back to my job as a waitress. We were starting to feel settled and happy again. A year went by—and then my husband decided to come back.

He wrote to the children and he wrote to me, saying how much he missed us, all the old charm, the promises. He had changed, he said; everything would be different, he was tired of Philadelphia and wanted to be with his family. I did not reply. I was afraid, and yet I wanted to see him.

One day, when I came back from work, he was there in the house with Nancy and Michael. He had just turned up, but he had had time to disrupt the happy home. Nancy was in tears. "He hasn't changed at all," she sobbed, "he's just like he was before."

My husband was being critical. "So this is the place you've got!" he scoffed . "I don't think much of it. Look at this junk", pointing to the furniture. "We can't live with that..." and so on. The familiarity of it made my heart sink. What could I do? We were all upset, confused, and a weary sense of hopelessness settled over me.

As it happened the owners of the house came back from Japan early so we had to move anyway. "Where are we going to live now?" I asked—but it was starting to feel like a routine, scouring newspaper adverts, calling estate agents at a time when private property was difficult to find. Eventually we rented a three-bedroom house not far from Burbank and my husband started going out for job interviews.

There was plenty of work for a man with his knowledge of precision tools, but he often came home angry because of the slights, real or imagined over his lack of army service. This, he shouted in despair and frustration, was exactly what he'd anticipated when he'd tried to leave his wartime job to join up. At one place, a sneering interviewer who'd lost a leg in the war came near to being hit for insinuating Michael was a draft-dodger. "He was sitting there as if he was a hero," Michael said. "I tried to tell him why I wasn't in the war but he wouldn't listen. He acted like I was a spy, then he said, 'At least you didn't have your leg shot off', and I just wanted to sock him one."

Michael eventually had a job with Litton's as an instrument-maker but by this time he was looking for insults and said that the other workers were condescending and he was going back to Pennsylvania where his expertise was appreciated.

I tried to calm him by telling him this sort of thing would soon wear off and he should ignore it. It was obviously the wrong thing to say because he exploded with anger, locked himself in the garage, and made such a din throwing things around that the neighbours complained to the police, who turned up and marched him off. He was released without charge.

Meanwhile the rest of us were putting down roots again. Nancy and young Michael were doing well at school, and a neighbour I met in the street urged me to join the Toastmistresses' Club. This turned out to be a huge addition to my life. My husband wouldn't let me invite friends home so the club was a good way of meeting people and having some social life. Of course he objected and said it was silly to join a group of gossiping women with nothing in their heads but I went ahead anyway.

My fellow toastmistresses were far from empty-headed. They were all interesting, professional women—a doctor, an architect, a physicist, and an inspiration to me. One of the things we did was to take turns to give talks. So apart from making good friends, I gave a talk about twice a month and learned to think and speak on my feet, which eventually I found very useful. For unknown to me then, it launched me on an exciting career as an art teacher which eventually took me to Europe, brought me fame on television and at last, a blissfully happy domestic life in England.

But that was still in the future.

For now, it was still a matter of survival, of scraping together money, and not being mentally crushed by my husband at home. It made things no easier that I loved Michael still, and I knew that he loved me. But survival can mean hard decisions, and when, after the garage incident involving the police, he decided to leave us again and go back to Philadelphia, I knew that this marriage was never going to work. Divorce was the only answer.

A friend in the toastmistresses married to a lawyer told me to go to him for help. I didn't have any money but Jerry said, "Never mind, just paint me a picture." He filed a divorce for me, and the decree would become absolute after a year of separation.

Nancy, my uncomplaining daughter and helper at home had graduated from high school and was now making her own life in Philadelphia. We kept closely in touch. My only financial responsibility left was young Michael, who had grown into a tall, strong teenager with a huge appetite, endless energy for basketball, and lots of friends like himself.

Throughout this period my toastmistress friends were a help and support. Through them I made contacts, sold pictures, had commissions to do portraits, and best of all, they lifted my spirits by liking my work. My "studio" was the far end of the kitchen—rather convenient because I could stir the pot at the same time as painting. The only risk was that at times of artistic enthusiasm I occasionally stirred the pot with the paintbrush.

I had one prestigious commission: a trio of two-by-three foot canvases, for the Pacific Coast Stock Exchange, "and nothing abstract" ordered the director. So I did some research and painted Wall Street in 1850; Chicago, and the Los Angeles Stock Exchange in 1899 with a group in the foreground looking remarkably like ( no wonder, I copied their photographs) the present directors.

They loved it, and the fee was just in time to tide me over till the next crisis. My problem was that I had no qualifications to do anything but paint; apart from selling my pictures I could only find badly-paid menial work and I needed regular money to pay the rent and food bills.

Shortage of money seems to have figured constantly in my life—perhaps it does in most people's—but I am a survivor. It had acted as a spur to numerous enterprises, yet now, even my optimism faltered.

I had been making a few dollars a day working at a hobby shop until the rather mousey husband of the woman who owned the place raided the till and did a runner with all the money. None of us workers was surprised. Madame was a bully and we reckoned she had it coming. It came on the heels of another robbery when I was standing at the cash register and a weasely-looking man with a gun staged a hold-up. I saw with shock the barrel of his gun uncomfortably close to my head as, on his orders, I stuffed notes into his bag, and my portrait-painter's eye took in the shape of his nose, his mouth, his scarred right ear. He grabbed the money, ran to the getaway car. "What sort of car?" the police demanded. "A blue one," I said. "It's make?" the policeman shouted. "And did you get the number?"

"No, but I could draw the man." So I did, and they got him. Nevertheless I lost my job, because after her husband took the rest of the money, the owner closed down.

Once again in the newspaper ads, I looked for work in vain, and at length was grateful to find four hours a day at Penny's Department Store selling in the lingerie department for 90 cents an hour. Not much, but far better than nothing.

I was describing my abortive attempts to get a job over a drink after one toastmistresses' meeting, when Iona said, "Nan, why don't you give us painting lessons? We'd pay."

" But I don't know if I could ," I said.

Another woman sitting nearby butted in. "Why don't you try? I'd go."

"So would I," her friend said. Before I left, I had eight potential students. So could I do it? As I walked home, I thought of the bills, the rent I owed, and I thought of the idea. Maybe. Yes, I could do it.

# Chapter 22

A plan started growing. I'd been to lots of art classes myself and seen students get discouraged and drop out after a few weeks. The teacher would pile some junk onto a table, tell the students to paint a still life, wander off and come back later and tell them what they should have done. They dropped off like flies. I thought I'd teach in a completely different way. Every student should go home with a picture she could be proud of, something she could hang on the wall and say, 'I did it.' That way they would keep their enthusiasm and I'd keep up my numbers.

I worked out a way to do it. First, I must show them exactly how to mix colours: not, "mix a little yellow with blue," but "take half a level teaspoon of Naples yellow, quarter a teaspoon of aqua, a smidge of cadmium orange…" Give a formula, like a recipe. And I'd teach them about tonal values. "Take a quarter teaspoonful of cadmium yellow. Divide into three piles. For the medium tone, leave as it is. For light tone, add three quarters teaspoonful of zinc white and half teaspoonful zinc yellow. For dark, add half teaspoonful yellow ochre." Then we would all paint the same picture, everyone using a grid on the canvas to follow me, and at the end of the lesson everybody would have a reasonably respectable picture to take home. Great art? No, I know it wasn't, but it would be enjoyable, and there was a product at the end. And the pupil would learn and possibly go on using new-found confidence to experiment and improve.

I was sure now that it could work—but as I'd need a studio and had no money to rent one, the whole thing seemed infeasible. At the next toastmistress's meeting, Ione said, "Well, when do you start the painting lessons?"

"I don't know," I said. "I haven't got a studio."

"We've worked that out," interrupted blonde Adelaide who was married to Harold and lived in a big house. "We'll use my garden room. Harold's always out on Wednesday evenings."

"And we'll bring our own easels," Ione added. "We pay in advance." So they'd got it all worked out. It was irresistible.

We started two weeks later with a picture of yellow marigolds in a blue vase. I showed it to the class, and they approved it; the flowers would match the drapes in her sitting room, Lesley added. We had from 7:30 to 10:30 before Harold came home.

"First, a thin wash of umber on the canvas; wipe it with a tissue," I began. "Now paint in the grid, five lines on the long side, three on the short side..." There was silence and concentration as nine brushes squared off nine canvases. We placed the position of the vase and moved on to the flowers. Adelaide glanced anxiously at the door. She and Harold were childless but they had a child-substitute, a Siamese cat called Ching who sat on top of a large cabinet in the studio and watched us lazily. At 10.30 Harold came home, put his head round the door, wished us a cheery good night and went to bed, our signal to pack up and go home. Everything had gone well, to my immense relief.

Next week, the full class was there raring to go. We finished the marigolds and started on a street scene of Montmartre, which I'd found in a travel brochure. By this time more women were asking to join and I had slightly changed the technique. I found the students were over-working the paint and making the colours look muddy, so I got them to use palette knives instead of brushes, which produced an instant improvement.

I was already starting to feel a little uneasy about using Adelaide's garden room as a studio because I sensed we finished too late in the evenings, when Ching the cat made a decisive move. We were finishing late again. Adelaide was a little edgy though she said nothing. I glanced up just in time to see the cat leap from the top of the cupboard right on to Jeanette's palette. She screamed. The cat slid on to the carpet, paws full of oil paint, and ran. Adelaide chased him, Harold came running down stairs in his pyjamas trying to pull on his trousers and the cat skittered across the wall-to-wall carpet leaving a trail of paint to the French doors. Harold was not pleased.

I told the bewildered and trembling Adelaide that we would find another studio for next week, as I helped her clean her carpet. Harold went back to bed. Edna, one of the pupils said we could switch to the rumpus room of her house.

Next week we turned up at Edna's. She was a widow with grown up children and did not often use her rumpus room. It seemed ideal—until we saw it: white walls, white ceiling, and immaculate snowy-white wall-to-wall carpet, which Edna had covered with a sheet of transparent plastic. We were so intimidated by the pristine perfection of it all, we found ourselves speaking in whispers and at the coffee break we drank from thin white china and ate dainty little cakes. The inevitable happened of course—a smudge of paint on the carpet despite the plastic, and I think Edna was much relieved when I told her we would have to find somewhere else for the next week.

I went home thinking. There was really only one thing I could do: clear out the sitting room in my own apartment and use it as a studio for the next four weeks, then take a break in June to look for a shed or something that I could rent and do up.

I broke the news to Michael over dinner. He and his friend Steve were putting away huge helpings of spaghetti, both over 6 ft tall now and hungry after basketball practise.

"You want to open a studio here, in this apartment?" Michael repeated. "You know Mom, I think you are becoming unhinged."

"Let her finish, Mike," Steve chipped in.

"I know I can make a good living," I said. "But I just need a place to tide us over to the end of term"

"But here! Are you serious? And what will you do next?" Michael was shouting.

"I'll find a studio to rent. I can get something cheap and do it up."

"Using what for money?" Michael demanded.

"I've got good credit, I can get a loan."

"Come on Mike. We can move the furniture for her into the dining area," Steve said. "Don't you worry Mom (all Mike's friends called me "Mom") we'll set it up for you."

For the next four weeks I squeezed all the students into our living room, where we were cramped but cheerful and everyone was enthusiastic about eventually having a proper studio of our own. But first I needed to borrow some capital.

I went to the bank confident of my gilt edge credit and good rating, but when I said I was divorced they said they could not lend me anything without collateral. So I cashed in my life insurance policy. The form said I needed my husband's signature so I found a sample signature among his papers and copied it. It looked all right to me and it looked all right to the staff at the insurance office, too. After all, I'd paid the premiums myself and there are times when you have to take a risk.

"You know, Ma, you're gambling our last cent on this studio idea," Michael complained. He still was not convinced it would work.

"Yes, and I'm going for broke." I was determined at least to give it a good try. "It's the only way I know of making a living."

It was mid summer and Michael was just graduating from high school. Grudgingly he conceded. "OK Ma, I'll drive you around to look for a place at the weekend. We'll soon find something suitable." But we didn't.

The first place we found did not have any toilet facilities. The nearest were a block away at a gas station. After a few weeks we were starting to feel discouraged when driving down a road in the evening about to go home, we came upon just the thing: a row of little shops and one of them was to let.

We peered through the shop window: the room was rather long and narrow, but that did not matter. The light was good, there was parking space in front and it was just a bus-ride from home—a consideration for me as a non-driver. We went and found the real estate agent , a big strapping man and he gave us the terms. They were very reasonable. ."Let's get it now," Michael urged. So I did. I gave the agent two months' rent in advance and we drove home happily and Michael spent the evening planning the studio. We could hardly wait to drive out in the morning. We had been there about 45 minutes when a terrible din broke out: a cacophony of barking, like a mad-house full of dogs. We ran outside just as a Porsche drew up in front of the shop next door and an expensive-looking woman got out carrying in her arms an even more expensive-looking pooch in a rhinestone collar. She entered the shop, which we now noticed was called "Clip Joint" and the barking crescendoed.

"I can never teach with all this noise," I cried. I'll tell the estate agent; we must get the money back. We did. He sounded resigned. It had happened before. He handed back our cheque and feeling disconsolate we started driving home.

Suddenly Michael stopped the car. "Nearly missed that," he said, reversing to a row of just four small shops, each with a rustic-looking porch over the front door and little unkempt gardens in front. There was a "for let" sign on one.

We found the estate agent on the board and drove around at once. Behind the desk was a spare, grey-haired woman who looked at us keenly and said in nasal voice that the rent was $75 a month and the "old man"—the owner, would deal with it tomorrow. "That your young-un?" she nodded towards my tall, skinny son as we turned to go. "He's going to be some man when he gets some meat on him." Michael, who can be sensitive about his height, grinned happily and we drove home, congratulating ourselves on having found the perfect place and crossing our fingers that the "old man" would not be a problem.

We met him the next morning. He was about 40 years old, a square-shaped man with a distracting habit of keeping his hands in his pockets and jingling his change. His office was next door. "I'm Ed Fogarty," he introduced himself. Clink, clink went the change. "That place been empty for a year." Clink clink. "Someone wanted to put fish and chips there. Too smelly. Then they wanted a Laundromat. Too much slish-sloshing." He grabbed a handful of change and cascaded it in his pocket. "And what do you want it for?"

"An art studio," I said. There won't be any noise, or smells—or anything…"

"Well, I dunno," he shook his head slowly. I froze. "Damn beatniks, those arty people…."

"Not these," I said hastily. "They are all women —like the Mayor of Burbank's wife…" I trailed off with some more name dropping.

"Well," he said slowly, "guess we could give it a try. Start with a month. I hope you make it. A lot of them artist-types starve, you know."

We hardly heard him. We were on cloud nine, light-headed with relief, dizzy with ideas. We took the key, inspected the new premises once more, saw the dirt, the broken bits of wood, the shambles of a long-unoccupied store, and in our mind's eye transformed it to the most perfect and smartest studio in California. We drove home to start on the plans.

# Chapter 23

We decided on black and white for the décor and Michael and I were there next day with the paint pots, slapping white over flesh-pink walls, sweeping out rubbish, pacing out the area for easels, stools and storage... Michael made pegboard panels for each side of the room to hold unfinished pictures and painted them bright colours against the white; and meanwhile I found 15 yards of black and white striped denim to make scalloped valances for the windows and salvaged a black candelabra and a dressing table to turn into a black desk.

The studio started to shape up. Our energy and frantic banging attracted the neighbours who came to look—first, our change-jingling landlord, Fogarty reminding me of a buck-toothed bunny, came offering footling advice at regular intervals, then Hank, the suave charmer from the other side who edited a magazine about dogs. "An art studio, eh?" he said. "In Burbank, eh? Well, we'll see which of us goes broke first."

Late in the evenings we went home too tired to for anything heavier than a bowl of spaghetti, and rose next day fresh for the assault.

My friends arrived to help. We had to go shopping for easels, stools, storage units for each student to hold paints and palettes… I was determined that this would be a smart studio: my students were not the kind to suffer for their art. At the local cut-price store I found a small metal table on wheels with a shelf below. "Eleven of those," I said to the astounded clerk. Then Iona and I went to the main art store for easels and examined their two grades: $5.95 for the collapsible lightweight, $25 for the solid up-market professional.

"We'd better get the cheap ones," Iona hissed.

I heard the prig-faced salesman sneer to his sidekick, "I've got a pair of Picassos here.".

"I'll take eleven of the best," I snapped at him. "No, make that a dozen." Meanwhile Michael was buying driftwood shutters for the windows and in the afternoon my friends Lucille and Iona started hoeing the weed-patch in front of the studio ready for planting geraniums.

It was very hot and Fogarty's wife Belle noseyed round. "I see you've got some whores outside," she said in her mid-west accent.

"Whores?" I was alarmed.

"That's right: whores." She made a hoeing gesture.

"Ah yes: Iona and Lucille…" I chortled to myself. A week later the "whores" helped me address 250 engraved invitations to all the local dignitaries and businessmen, names and addresses furnished by Iona the wife of Burbank's Mayor, for the grand opening of an art studio.

By this time it not only looked like something picked from a homes-and-gardens magazine, complete with a dozen black-lacquered rush-seated Italian stools (courtesy of a loan from Lorna's husband) but the whole row of four shops shone under a fresh coat of black and white paint—Fogarty's contribution to operation spruce-up, for which he later won the "Burbank Beautiful" municipal award for the most improved business property in town.

Everyone was happy. It was the end of a hot, busy summer and Michael and I had just $25 left in the bank. Our friends donated a case of champagne, we all dressed up to the nines and the Cadillac and Thunderbird crowd rolled up. The mayor was in his finery, husbands being affable; students in their jewellery, bright red lipstick and tottering heels were photographed by the local newspaper. Old Fogarty was much impressed to see that these artists did not look as if they starved in garrets. The following week, classes started.

It was a fresh chapter in my life. At last some sort of security seemed in reach, and with it came a lively run of drama and incidents that still make me laugh. Warm and generous friendships from those days have followed me through the years.

I had two daily sessions: three hours in the morning, three in the afternoon, and the numbers grew. Oh, the relief of the steady income. Michael was able to go to college where he had a basketball scholarship, my daughter Nancy was working in a bank in Philadelphia, and my husband was almost an "ex".

To expect things to go that smoothly was perhaps unrealistic and I was not entirely surprised when my husband wrote and said he wanted to come back.

The year's separation needed for our divorce to become final was not yet up. One part of me wanted to see him again— and yet experience and common sense told me it would not work. Feeling confused and uncertain I went, as I often had as a child, to the priest who advised me that my husband needed psychiatric help and he should get it before I let him return. I remembered the man I had fallen in love with, the kind and responsible husband who ungrudgingly took my young sisters into our home, the father who loved his children, and wrote to him giving the conditions.

He kept his side of the bargain. He went to a psychiatrist, had treatment in hospital, and then he came back home. He seemed better. I was happy to see him and hoped that the depression, the unpredictable anger and silences were over. But his demons had not yet finished with him.

When my hopes had risen and I was thinking I could keep us with the studio until he was quite well, he took me for a long walk and explained, more lucidly than I ever remember before that he had to go away again, and this time for good.

I cried and begged him not to. He said, "I'm no good for you. I can't support a family. You are able to earn your own living and people like you. You can get on better without me."

I realised with heavy sadness that this really was the end of our marriage. Back at home he loaded his books into the car and packed a few clothes while I stayed upstairs. When he was ready to go he called out, "Nan, are you coming down to say goodbye to me?" Drained of feeling and with no tears left I realised that for the first time in all the years I was married to him I felt absolutely nothing for him any more. If I hadn't been able to help him through his depressions and moods in 25 years I could not do it now. So I shouted from the window, "No I'm not and I never want to see you again as long as I live." He shrugged and drove off. This time it was the end. I divorced him.

Now that chapter was out of the way, my new life bounded forward. There was no room for regret, no time for introspection. "The Sunday Painters of Burbank" (the classes were actually midweek) were about to take off and it needed all my time and energy to keep ahead.

# Chapter 24

The Sunday Painters may have been rank amateurs but they also had their dreams. Every class was full of laughter; we had coffee breaks, cigarettes were hurriedly put out and windows fanned open before the fire officer called, then re-lit when he had gone—but through it all ran periods of intense concentration and silence when everyone was lost in the creation of their art.

Between lessons I worked out the next pictures. As before, we drew the grids, washed the canvases in burnt umber, mixed paints to a formula, applied them with palette knives. When "real artists"—who included my son at Art College—said it was not "real art", all I could say was that it worked. When we painted an apple it looked like an apple. Some ten years later in Britain, when I was doing the HTV programme Paint Along With Nancy, my "instant art" sessions honed in Burbank won a huge following and the series ran for three years.

Although everyone did the same pictures, there was diversity within the rules. Some of my pupils painted with wild slashes of colour. Mary Ann insisted (admittedly against my advice, but it was her picture) on painting in extreme detail, trees leaf by leaf, grass blade by blade. As for Elaine, she surprised us all.

She had become quite a good painter.

It was November, and we decided to be seasonal and paint a pot of poinsettias for Christmas. I decided to try an impressionist approach because we were all using palette knives instead of brushes by this time.

"Do you think we'll finish them by December 15?" Elaine asked. " We're having a Christmas party; my husband's invited his new boss. I want to have my picture hanging in the sitting room. "

"Impasto takes a long time to dry, and red's a slow-drying pigment," I warned her.

Elaine finished ahead of time and had the beautifully painted poinsettias framed while still wet, to hang on her wall, where it was much admired by the boss's wife. In fact the boss's wife wanted to buy it.

"Oh, no," said Elaine, who was very fond of her pictures and kept them all.

"Please!" said boss's wife, playfully unhooking it from the wall and hugging it to her blond mink coat. Elaine's shout of warning was too late. The boss's wife was wearing the only red mink coat in Burbank, and it did not really suit her.

Meanwhile after class Jeanette had taken her painting out to the car balancing it on the palm of her hand like a pie. I had started cleaning up the studio when she raced back looking very agitated.

"I've lost it," she said. "The picture! I must have put it on the roof of the car and forgotten it was there. I can't remember the streets I drove down."

"I'll look with you," I said. We closed up the studio and drove off.

We didn't have to go far before we saw the picture on the wet road, face up. It had been run over several times. Jeanette picked it up with dismay. "But it looks quite interesting like that," I said to cheer her up. "A kind of Jackson Pollock effect.

You should enter it for the All City Art Exhibition." She did, and it was accepted. What's more, it won the Best of Show prize. The local newspaper gave her an enthusiastic and erudite review praising her "impression of flowers painted as if observed from several viewpoints by the blending together of the various areas of brilliant colour." We all laughed our heads off.

There was always much laughter in the classes and with new friendships and expanding work, the old fears and insecurities drifted into the distance. Incidents, and there were plenty of them, were usually funny, at least in retrospect. Like the day Mr Beadle turned up with Mr Dudley.

Mr Beadle was a small, thin man with a serene expression, in his late fifties. Mr Dudley was his grey, stringy dog with hair hanging over its eyes.

Mr Beadle said he would like to buy one of the seascape paintings we had just been doing. I took them down and we began discussing them. I asked Mr Beadle if he would like some coffee. He politely declined, but said that Mr Dudley would take some.

My friend Kate who had been helping me clean up the studio poured the dog some coffee. Mr Beadle narrowed the seascapes down to two, turned to the dog and said, "And Mr Dudley, which do you prefer?"

"Don't make up your mind now, Mr Beadle," I said hastily. "Why don't you and Mr Dudley discuss it and let me know tomorrow?" By this time I was rather anxious to get rid of him and Kate could hardly hide her mirth.

The pair of them left, and I was starting to put the seascapes back when the door was flung open and a barrel-chested man with a red face staggered in roaring, "I wanna see yer etchings," shouting with laughter.

"We're closed. Come back tomorrow," I said.

"Got any nudes? You ain't no artist. I'll paint you nude, baby " he yelled. He made a grab at me. Just then Mr Beadle and Mr Dudley came back in.

"Help!" I shouted.

Brave Mr Beadle ran at the gorilla and tried to hit him. The gorilla swatted him to the ground and Mr Beadle slid across the floor, out for a count.

"Get him Dudley," I shouted but the dog yawned and settled down to rest.

I managed to grab an open tin of paint, which I slung at the gorilla's face, and he staggered back shouting with paint in his eyes. I shoved him out and locked the door, and he made such a racket shouting and kicking it that a neighbour called the police who came, sirens wailing, and took him away in a van.

Mr Beadle was not badly hurt. He got to his feet and I thanked him for bravely coming to help me. "Not like your dog," I couldn't resist adding.

Mr Beadle patted the animal's mangy head. "Mr Dudley abhors violence, don't you friend?" he said. I offered Mr Beadle coffee with a tot of anisette which I kept in the studio for emergencies. As he sipped it, he said, "I came back to tell you that after discussing it with Mr Dudley, we decided not to buy the seascape for now."

After that, the couple were weekly visitors to the studio. They were still interested in the picture. I would excuse myself and clear up while they discussed it. Eventually, when I went to live in Rome two years later, I gave Mr Beadle the painting.

The classes rolled on into the spring and we held an exhibition and sold some paintings. A few men joined and by now I had 55 students. Then the numbers started to fall off. I hadn't reckoned with the summer holidays. Soon it was clear that for a month or so there would be no point in having classes at all. By July, with just one class a week I was back with the old problem of how to make enough money to pay for food and the rent.

Michael was now sharing a flat with college friends and he found a part time job that helped with his college expenses. My daughter was still working in Philadelphia. During the slow summer months I painted small items for gift shops, had a few portrait commissions, and an unusual one—to paint a piano.

The piano, an old-fashioned upright that had been in the family for years, belonged to my friend Gwen. She lived on a ranch in Chatsworth where her retired husband bred horses- one of them, an insignificant-looking dappled grey munching docilely in the stall was the winner of a number of high-profile races and still going strong. Gwen was more interested in her piano.

It had brass candleholders bracketed to the front, and fret-work scrolls backed with dingy green cloth. The woodwork was in quite a mess and Gwen wanted me to paint it in black and gold as I had done the furniture in the studio.

I stripped down the wood and sealed it, then put on the paint. It was an enjoyable job and the piano looked a lot better, shining black with gold leaf scroll decorations and old gold cloth behind the fretwork.

Gwen was pleased with the result. She came to my painting class and chatting afterwards over a cup of coffee she said she was arranging a 29-day tour of Europe for the Los Angeles County Art Museum of which she was a patron.

"I've signed you on to come too," she said. "It isn't until next September."

"What? But I can't afford it!" I was aghast. Not only did I not have the money, but also with the studio closed for a month over summer again I would not be earning anything.

"You can make it," she said, unruffled. "You can raise some by raffling your pictures. You've got wall-to-wall paintings and 55 students. Sell them the canvases one by one. Charge a dollar a ticket."

Without her chivvying I wouldn't have had the gall, but there were seven months to raise the money and we did it. In fact I raised twice the fare, which gave me money for spending, too. I was jubilant. And my students were delighted. "Operation Europe" was now on.

I had been living on my own for the first time in my life and not much liking it. Both my children were away finding their own independence and I had been feeling flat, my life slowing down. It needed a good kick to get going again. Emotionally the timing was perfect for an adventure in Europe, seeing the magnificent Renaissance art of Italy, and gradually I assembled a more daring agenda.

What if I could get a job teaching art in Italy and stay there for a whole year? Maybe it was my Italian blood, but I felt that if only I could go to Rome, I would feel wonderfully at home; surrounded by the paintings, the sculpture and infused by the culture that had been ever-present in my childhood. It was an impossible dream of course, but worth a try.

Time spent on reconnaissance is rarely wasted, as the general said and I got going with some advance work on finding a job in Europe and sounding out the territory.

There was an American naval base in Naples. I wondered if they needed someone to teach painting there? A far hope, perhaps, but you never know.

I wrote to a friend's brother in Washington, who said to write to the Chief of Navy Personnel in Washington, and after doing that I wrote to my Congressman asking him to put in a word for me , and eventually, to my incredulous joy came back a letter saying an appointment had been made for me to meet Lieutenant Adam Foreman at the naval base in Naples in October. My optimism, never long below par surged back.

I told Gwen about my plan. "So when we get to Amsterdam, I'll leave the rest of the party and take a train to Naples. Yes, I know I've never been outside the United States before but I know I can manage. And I'm going to get one of those Euro Rail passes. First I'll go to Paris, and Venice on the way to Naples, and stop off at little hotels, then I'll travel on to Rome and spend a week there and I'll meet you all back in Amsterdam to fly home to California." It sounded easy—but I started to feel a bit apprehensive as the time drew near, and bought a hat pin for protection. Michael and Nancy both thought I was off my head to even think of working in Italy. "At your age, Mom? Are you mad? You'll be glad to get back home." They didn't really take it seriously.

Foggarty, his wife Belle and Hank took me out for a farewell lunch, friends gave me endless advice, some of it quite useful, and on September 19 the members of the Los Angeles County Art Museum and I flew off into the night. We landed in Amsterdam just after midnight the next day, jet-lagged, tired, ready to drop asleep and were distributed among three different hotels by the tour agent.

I awoke at eleven next morning, fresh and with the aroma of coffee rising from the cafe below. Patterned sunlight filtered through lace curtains onto a snow-white embroidered bed cover and I gazed around enchanted by the old world decor of the room. Downstairs in the pavement cafe there were hot crusty rolls for breakfast and a big cup of coffee with hot milk and I lazily watched people walking and bicycling down the street. There were far more bicyclists than cars. It was peaceful, unhurried, and if this was Europe, I liked it.

I said goodbye to the rest of the Los Angeles County Art Museum party and with a delicious sense of freedom and excitement, I booked in for another night at the hotel and decided to take the train to Bruges and Paris next day.

# Chapter 25

After breakfast I walked to the tourist office to plan my itinerary and book tickets. I felt like a nineteenth century traveller on the grand cultural tour, except that mine was on a cheese-paring budget and I planned to travel at night, sleeping on trains to save the cost of hotels.

After changing currency I bought sandwiches and a bar of chocolate to eat on the journey to Bruges next day, and put them in my bag. I would change trains in Belgium and go straight to Paris, because as Oscar Wilde said, all good Americans go to Paris and I had to see the Louvre and the Madeleine and everything.

Meanwhile I was a child on Christmas morning, excited, full of anticipation, senses sharpened and a bit scared. When I shut my eyes I could smell fresh coffee, anise, the canals, scents of a different continent and when I listened I heard the soft sound of bicycle tyres on the road instead of motors.

The day passed like a happy dream, half jet-lagged, and next day, late in the evening, I left for Belgium.

The sound of the guards checking passports as we crossed the frontier woke me up. And again came the little jerk of excitement as I looked out of the window and saw shadowy church spires and the glint of water on the canals.

There was just time for a tour of the city before going on to Paris, a few hours to explore the narrow cobbled streets and the great gothic cathedral. And there was just time, perhaps, for a meal at a sidewalk cafe, a glass of wine, and a salad But there had not been time. I missed my connection and waited hours for the night train to Paris, resolving to be more disciplined in future.

As dawn broke we slid into the Gare du Nord, and I towed my suitcases to the Jeanne d'Arc, a family pension where I was given a dingy room with a lumpy bed, but where I forgave all when that evening Madame slammed the food down on the long communal table: vegetable soup, boeuf bourguignon, a huge bowl of salad and a flask of red vin de table.

Meanwhile, I did the sights. I walked the streets, the galleries, the parks, along the river and into the churches. I needed months, not hours and, as I took the train on to Basle, I resolved, as one does, to go back soon to see the rest.

In Switzerland I had my first taste of romance, European style. It was not at all Hollywood. I sat on the bench in the town square where there was a patch of grass, a few market stalls and a little cafe with a red-cheeked woman in peasant dress serving the sort of food that reminded me this was no longer France.

"This place looks like a picture in a story book," I was thinking to myself contentedly. And right on cue came, not exactly the prince, but a tall man with brown, grey-flecked hair, a plain but agreeable face and wearing a very smart suit. In fact I'd noticed him staring at me half an hour earlier in the cafe when I was having coffee. He gave a little bow and asked permission to sit on the bench. I nodded.

"The weather is gutt," he said.

"Yes," I agreed.

"You are American," he said.

"Yes".

"I worked in America two years," he said. "I am an engineer."

"Oh", I said. This conversation so far was not lively.

"You are a woman on your own?" he asked, looking at me as if trying to work out my age. "A widow perhaps? Divorced?"

"Widow", I said.

The wrong answer. He took my hand, gazed into my eyes and said,.

"I want to marry you."

I was speechless. He continued, "I do not like Switzerland. I do not like my work. I do not like the women here, they are dull. They dress badly," he added as a robust woman in a trench coat, flat walking shoes and a felt hat with a feather in it strode by.

"I'm sorry, Mr, er," I said.

"Brandt. Peter Brandt."

"I'm afraid I'm engaged to be married."

He never did know my name, but he gave me his visiting card in case I changed my mind, and left me reflecting ruefully that my green eyes, my gipsy black hair and scarlet lipstick were as nothing compared to an American passport. Later, when I was living in Rome, I met two American widows who had had similar offers and taken them up. One marriage was a disaster and the other was surprisingly happy.

In the late afternoon I had to board the train again, this time for Venice.

Much as I like train journeys, by now I was in need of a good night's sleep in a proper hotel bed; but by the time the train arrived at 9pm, the station tourist office was closed and I stood disconsolate with my big suitcase wondering where to turn.

"Hotel?"

A small thin man in crumpled clothes was speaking to me. Of course I should have said "No", but I said "Yes". I was desperately tried. He grabbed my suitcase and staggered off with it barely skimming the ground, while I followed carrying my small case. He hurried across the piazza to a waiting motor launch, jumped aboard and handed me in, and I felt, mingled with fear a sudden thrill of excitement. There were other passengers in what I realised was a water taxi but when the thin man indicated it was our turn to get off, my excitement turned to unease. And then downright fear as he hurried ahead of me down narrow cobbled streets lit only with little patches of light from wrought iron lanterns hanging from the buildings.

All I heard was the drip of water and the footfalls of my guide. He turned, shifted the case, and beckoned me to hurry. At every corner I hesitated and he beckoned me on.

In about fifteen minutes we emerged from the gloom into a beautiful piazza, lights, an ornate doorway, a glass door, La Fenice, one of the best-known hotels in Venice. My guide put my suitcase in the lobby, turned round and vanished as a smooth concierge came up and asked in perfect English, "Would you like a room, madam?"

"What will this cost?" I wondered as I nodded. There are times when money does not matter and I was weak with relief. Moments later the porter unlocked a door on the second floor and put my suitcase in the lobby of a room, which made me, gasp with delight.

It was long and narrow, the floor tiled and the furniture elegant. I ran to the window, opened the shutters, and gazed at a panoramic view, like a stage set, balconies, with flowers and Madonnas, buildings with ochre plaster peeling to show warm pink bricks beneath. And there was silence but for the sound of soft footsteps and quiet voices drifting up from the piazza. I was in love with the place.

When dawn broke, the sense of romance was still there, in the musty smell of dampness from the canals, reflections of ancient palaces moving and sparkling on the water, and the gondoliers and tour guides who played it for all it was worth.

Mario Caruso was our guide. We were a small group and he led us around the A-list of sights: St Mark's Square, the Dodge's Palace, and the Bridge of Sighs

Caruso was dark, clean-shaven, about two inches short of six foot and he wore a jacket with ferocious shoulder padding that made him look like a bruiser. That impression was strengthened by a broken nose and an unusual tiptoe walk, like a boxer dodging round an opponent in the ring.

At the end of the day he took me aside and said he would like to show me Venice at night—how about coffee and a drink in St Mark's Square? It sounded like a perfect finale.

I dressed up, sophisticated, elegant, with a subtle veil of perfume, I murmured thanks to his compliments and wondered why he hadn't found someone more his own age. A soft evening breeze blew in from the grand canal and we sat beneath one of the most beautiful cathedrals of the world listening to music. He took my hand and gazed into my eyes. "Is beautiful, no?" he said. "Yes," I whispered. I must have had too much red wine.

"When I met you something go 'click'. I think, such a beautiful lady, without an escort. But I am an artist also, and I know all artists like to be alone."

"But I am not alone. I have an art school of 29 pupils in California."

"So you understand," Caruso murmured, gently squeezing my hand. "An artist must work to eat, to dress, to go to the cinema."

I'm not sure why the cinema rated so highly as a basic need in his life but I got the drift. Money. And I was an American, which meant I must have it. At that moment a gondola hung over-all with lanterns glided by and from it rose the voice of a tenor singing an aria from Tosca. I clapped and Caruso laughed.

"Is romantic, no?" he said happily. We strolled back to the hotel where he kissed my hand and said "Buona notte." As I left next morning for Rome he slipped a little billet doux into my hand. I read it on the train. It was a request in tortured English for money for the Artists' Workshop of Venice.

When I arrived in Rome in the afternoon, I booked into an hotel right in the centre, near the Piazza Republica. It was called the Texas Pensione, but was run by a well-fed Italian American who had gone native and whose own round girth was an advertisement to the pasta and rich red wine of his tables.

Nobody can see the Eternal City in two days, but if it had been possible the guide who led a tour from the pensione would have done it. Ex-Army, I supposed, seeing the ramrod figure clad in a black suit and felt hat, a baton in his hand. He used the stick to keep his flock in line, raising it with a shout, "Avanti!" turning on his heel with the precision of a drill sergeant and pointing ahead with a roar of "Prrrego!" We, mainly Americans, marched smartly behind, no time to loiter, to the Spanish steps, the Pantheon, the Trevi fountain,

"If it's Monday this must be Rome". The old joke came back to me as I embarked on the train again, on to Sorrento, Pompeii, Capri and—the reason for my breakaway from the Los Angeles County Art Museum party—an appointment at the Naples American Naval Base with Lieutenant F. for the post of recreational art teacher.

The train got to Naples mid-morning and I looked for the tourist office at the station but, unusually, there did not seem to be one. Maybe I looked lost, for hardly two minutes passed before a man with curly hair and a thin moustache came up and asked if I wanted an hotel or to go to Capri.

"To Capri, I said, "and Sorrento and Pompeii. And I'll need an hotel as well." Following a tout had worked in Venice so I as not perturbed when this one swept up my suitcase and staggered across the street with it. But I was a little taken aback when he went into a dingy shop that bore a large sign, "The Paradise Travel Agency." The name itself sounded suspicious especially as the inside looked more like the other place. It was, I thought charitably, a little run down.

Never mind, so long as they deliver the goods. The tout spoke to the boss. The boss turned to me. "Capri?" he said. "Today?"

"Yes."

He turned to the only other customer in the shop, a Scotsman, as it turned out, and said, "Can this lady go with you?" The Scotsman declined.

"Never mind, I find you another car," said Enrico the boss, "and you go to Pompeii first, then Sorrento then Capri. It take two days."

I checked my room reservation at a hotel for when I got back, and mentioned to Enrico my "important engagement" at the US naval base for the day after, as surety against trouble. Not that I expected any.

An hour later I was in the car with Luigi the tout driving. I'd left my big suitcase in the hotel and took only a small travelling bag containing my jewellery, money and a change of clothing and off we spun into the dry southern countryside, the sun slanting through vineyards and onto terra cotta roofs, Luigi pointing out features of interest. We stopped at a pretty trattoria for lunch. Luigi said he was not hungry and wandered off and when I finished I went to the car to find him.

What I saw made me freeze. He had opened the back and was trying to unzip my case. Luckily the zip had stuck—it always does—and he was frantically trying to get it open.

"What are you doing with my case?" I shouted.

He jumped. "I get my jacket," he stammered.

"From my suitcase?"

He was shaking. "I see your case open so I try to shut it. Now I go and pay for lunch."

When he came back we did not mention the matter again but I kept an eye on him while he became extra attentive and pretended nothing had happened.

At Pompeii he came round and opened my door. I got out—and saw at the entrance to the ruins two men standing as if they were waiting for us. Luigi was nervous. He kept glancing over his shoulder and his movements were jumpy. Suddenly I took fright.

"I don't want to stay here," I said. "Take me back."

"But Signora" Luigi reached out to grab my arm. I pulled away and shouted, "Take me back or I'll call those policemen." There were two of them across the piazza, and I shouted, "Police!"

"All right, please Signora, I take you back." Luigi was thoroughly alarmed. He shoved me into the car and slammed the door, but the policemen had noticed and came over to speak to him. He was blustering. One policeman made a note of his licence number and walked around the car. The other came round to my window and asked, "Tutto bene, Signora?"

"Si." I nodded.

Luigi looked shaken when he got back into the car. He accelerated off with a roar of the engine, tyres throwing up grit and I sat in tight silence till we reached The Paradise Tourist Agency.

I was not only frightened, but when I went back into the shambolic showroom I was angry as well. I told the boss Enrico that his guide had tried to go through my case, so I was cancelling the tour and wanted my money back. Luigi tried to defend himself and as tout and boss argued loudly in Italian I caught the word "police". Enrico's temperature was rising. He could do without the police in Paradise. So he hastily gave me back the money minus the cost of lunch and part of the journey and I went to my hotel.

The concierge was not surprised. He said he had "heard things" about The Paradise Tourist Agency. I arranged a tour of Capri for the next day from the hotel still feeling nervous. So this time I took the hatpin I had packed for dangerous occasions, and tucked it under the collar of my dress. But I did not need it.

Michele the guide was a dark, dapper man in a beige linen suit; handsome, I thought, and with such blue eyes one could not help noticing them. Having gathered his group of ten tourists in the bus, he sat beside me at the back and chatted in excellent English, which he said he taught at a school in Naples.

At Sorrento we walked by the orange and lemon groves, and made our way to the port to take the boat to Capri. There, to my surprise I saw the Scotsman who had been leaving The Paradise Tourist Agency just before me the previous day.

"Hello!" he shouted, and came over. "You know that tourist guide I went off with? He stole everything from my case, my money, travellers' cheques, the lot, then he cleared off and left me on a deserted road." So I had been right. I told him what had happened to me before we parted again, for my boat to Capri had arrived.

I boarded and, as the ferry approached the beautiful isle over clear water and I saw the rocky coast draped in sub tropical plants, I thought of Miss McNichol, our neighbour in Pennsylvania who had lent me her books and filled my childhood imagination with stories about this part of Italy.

When we disembarked Michele collected his group. We took the bus along precipitous roads to Anacapri where today the views attract visitors from the world as once they drew the emperors of ancient Rome.

My room in Anacapri seemed to hang over the sea and from it I could see the whole sweep of the bay. I had never seen anything more beautiful in my life and I felt that after three generations of exile from Italy the yearning for this land was still in my genes.

Tomorrow was the day I had planned and worked for: the vital meeting with Lieutenant F. whom I hoped would give me the job at the naval base. I had beaten the path: had the letter from my Congressman and from the naval personnel department in Washington.

Some of our tourist group stayed in Capri but I had to get back. Michele the guide came too. He sat next to me in the bus again. He put his hand on my knee. I moved to another seat. He moved over. I had to laugh: he was twenty years younger than me and he only came up to my chin. "Tomorrow evening when you come back I will see you again," he promised.

By now just one thing was on my mind: to get the job at the naval base in Naples so that I could come back to live in Italy. I telephoned to confirm the appointment. Yes, Lieutenant F. was expecting me. I took my letters of reference and at the base was escorted to the lieutenant's office. He greeted me warmly, a boyish-looking young man with a slightly petulant expression, but smart and relaxed in his uniform. He extended a hand and I noticed an expensive class ring, the high-school graduate's identity-tag in gold.

"So you want to work as a recreational art teacher?" he said. "Why Naples? I don't know that an art programme would go down well in the base here."

"My technique works," I protested. "I've got these letters of reference."

"You don't understand," he said. "Naples is hell. What the men want is beer, not art. They'd die laughing at you."

"So why are you interviewing me" I was incredulous.

"Well you seem to have good contacts and I want to get out of here. You were travelling in Italy anyway, I thought you might as well call in."

I was too devastated even to be furious. "You'll never know what it cost me to come here," I said.

He tried to be contrite. "Sorry if I misled you." He extended a hand again; his class ring caught the light—and I went back to my hotel with shattered dreams.

I was sitting there feeling depressed when Michele called. "Cheer up," he said, "You must come with me to the Bay of Naples and then to the national museum,. You can not leave without seeing them."

I felt too flat to refuse, and anyway, he was right. The streets of Naples were crowded, full of sound and colour, strings of lemons hanging in shop windows, vendors selling glow worms from trays, music from a hurdy-gurdy and market stalls, then the beauty of the bay and of the sculpture in the museum pushed my disappointment into the background.

Next day I had a farewell lunch with Michele in a cafe near the hotel, and to my utter astonishment, with the coffee came my second proposal of marriage.

"I could teach English, you could teach art". Michele was looking dreamy. I must have looked in shock.

"I'm not divorced yet," I lied.

"Never mind, we could just live together, no?"

"No," I said.

"I know what you think. Just because I am not a big man like Hercules (we had just seen the statue in the museum) you think I am not all man, eh? You will see"

Horrified, I felt myself blushing. He was delighted. "I knew that was the problem. I will call for you tonight in my new Ferrari, and now I take you back to your hotel."

He grabbed my arm tightly and as we walked I felt like the Queen Mary being escorted by a tugboat.

As soon as he had gone I asked the concierge for the time of the next train to Rome. "It goes in 45 minutes," he said.

I paid my bills, quickly wrote a note of regret to Michele saying I had to leave "due to unforeseen circumstances" and handed it to the concierge to deliver, then I grabbed my suitcase and taxied to the station.

I was back at the Texas Pensione in Rome a night early, but it gave me more time to explore and there was still too much to see. Next day I went to the Vatican. Afterwards I went to the coliseum.

"Be careful," warned the concierge at the hotel. "Tourists have been robbed at the coliseum." So I tucked the hatpin under my lapel just in case.

There were not many tourists around as I climbed the stone tiers of the massive amphitheatre. I was thinking about the hideous cruelties that had taken place in this spot when I felt a tug on my purse. I hung on and turned. There was a man, who said something in Italian. No one else was around. Covertly I took the hatpin from my lapel, and as he made another grab at my purse I jabbed it into his arm. He gave a yelp and I ran, followed by him, down steps, to the next level, where to my relief there were a couple of tourists. They turned as I shouted, "Help! He's trying to steal my purse!" The thief, seeing he was out-numbered, cleared off in a hurry.

My rescuers, a British couple escorted me still shaking with fright to a taxi and I returned to the pensione.

It was nearly time to make my way back to Amsterdam to meet up with the Los Angeles Art Museum group and to go home to America. There was one evening left.

Nervous though I still felt, I had to go out to eat because the pensione only served breakfast. I had heard of the Piazza Navone. Everyone said it was a place not to be missed, with its Bernini fountain, water tumbling over sculptured figures, the musicians and artists and cafes. So I took the bus and despite the piazza's reputation, was unprepared for its carnival liveliness and symmetrical beauty. Little did I know that one day it would become the place I called home and that I would live in mediaeval rooms just round the corner for nearly twenty years. I only knew then, as I gazed at it, that one day I would come back. Meanwhile I decided to take one last look at Paris on my way back to Amsterdam airport, and to stay overnight there to get a good night's sleep before the long flight home.

A mother and daughter at the pensione recommended a small hotel in Paris and I booked a room for next day. It was cold and wet when I arrived at 10pm and the taxi driver helped me with my suitcase into the lobby. But there had been a muddle. There was no room available.

The taxi driver shrugged. I looked, and felt, desperate. Where could I go? The driver asked the receptionist, who suggested another small hotel and off we went.

The place, when we found it, did not look much on the outside but I was grateful for anything. Inside, it looked even worse: dingy, musty, heavy with the smell of stale tobacco. A hard-faced receptionist with bright red lips and heavily mascaraed eyes sat sullenly behind a counter and eyed me with dislike. There was a chain around the waist of her black-beaded dress from which keys dangled. She offered no help as I dragged my suitcase up the narrow stairs; unhooked a key from her belt, handed it to me without a word and went back down.

The room lit by one bulb in the centre of the ceiling was cold and dirty and I decided to sleep with my clothes on. I took off my wet coat, put on an extra sweater and lay down exhausted.

I would have fallen to sleep straight away but for the noise: people clattering up and down the wooden stairs all night, and laughing and talking.

There was a knock on my door. I jumped off the bed, opened it a crack and a drunken sailor tried to push his way in. I shoved him back out and slammed the door to a stream of abuse. Later on, more banging on the door. I opened it an inch with my foot jammed against the bottom and squinted through the gap then slammed and barred it to another yell of anger from outside.

Maybe exhaustion had fogged my brain, but by this time I realised I was in a brothel. I sat fully clad on the bed and waited for dawn to break, and as soon as I dared, crept down to the receptionist, or more accurately, the Madam, to pay my bill and be off. She looked at the travellers' cheques and waved them away. She wanted cash. As surety, she shoved my suitcase under her counter.

I dashed out to change a cheque into francs but there was no bank or bureau de change round, so I hurried into a cafe and ordered coffee and a brioche. They would not change a travellers' cheque either. So I ran to a shoe shop and bought a pair of shoes that didn't fit. They changed the cheque; I ran back to the cafe and paid the bill then to the brothel to pay off the Madam and retrieve my baggage. And with huge relief I hailed a taxi and was just in time to catch the train for Amsterdam.

The rest was easy. I arrived at the airport early and slept a few hours snuggled into a corner in the warmth and safety of the waiting lounge until the Los Angeles County Art Museum tour group arrived like a sudden breeze with greetings and hugs and stories of adventures, but none to match my night in the Paris brothel. An hour later with a feeling of deep contentment we clipped on our safety straps and were lifted off for home.

# Chapter 26

I reopened the art studio in November and relished being back in Burbank where the familiar roads lined with palms, orange and lemon trees are broad and quiet, so different from the noisy street life of Rome. And I was happy to see my friends and students again, laughing about my adventures in Italy. "Trouble is, these Europeans think all American broads abroad must be rich," Brian joked. "Husbands making the dough, wives bored, Signor Handsome-But-Broke only too ready to help." We loaded our palette knives with rich, Mediterranean colours and the room reverberated with good-humoured teasing and gossip. I joined in, but nobody knew my secret: that I was going to go back. Back to Rome. And not for a holiday, but to live.

I was now in my fifties and did not have any money. My living was the studio. Could a woman in her fifties pack up her life like a gap-year student packing a rucksack, move from the New World to the Old and start another life from scratch? Crazy, of course. I had no friends or contacts in Italy; nowhere to live, my only two words of the language were "si" and "signor"- oh, and "pasta" of course—and no savings.

Then I looked around and saw the alternative: teaching, a few lectures to Burbank business clubs, tomorrow and the next day, and the next day. No, I'd rather be adventuring in Rome. But then I'd miss my family and friends. But then, having tasted the ancient beauty of Italy shouldn't I go there while physically I could? I argued this way and that. Then I decided to ask God.

I didn't expect quite such a prompt answer.

It was Thursday; luckily the end of my week's teaching for I had a bad headache and was lying on the divan. It was half-light, and I sensed someone's presence. I opened my eyes, and saw my ex-husband. He looked thin, wretched, there was sweat on his forehead and his eyes stared. I moved and he made as if to strike me. "If you are going to kill me, go ahead," I said, my head throbbing. "I'd sooner that than live with you again."

"You are my wife," he shouted.

"Your ex-wife. We are divorced."

He rampaged up and down the room banging his fist in his hand, shouting that I had destroyed his life, he couldn't trust anyone, he was going to kill himself—a threat he had made before—then he went. I felt emotionally exhausted. Would he keep coming back? Would I never be free of the madness and violence that had been so much part of my life? I comforted myself that after three years' absence he did not know where the two children were and decided that his return was a very good reason for my going to live in Rome.

So the decision had been made. I would have to tell my students, and Michael and Nancy. As it happened Michael was coming home for the weekend. It was November, the weather starting to get cold and wet and he was not in the best of moods because his car was falling to bits. He was in a considerably worse mood when I said I could not spare him money to buy another one because I was saving to move to Rome in July.

He was dumbfounded.

"You are a very selfish mother" he shouted, adding some observations about my age, my Italian vocabulary, the state of my mind.

Well maybe I should have found some other way of telling him, but I was angry too so I reached up and slapped him. He put his fist through the wall, which must have hurt because he had tears in his eyes when he rounded on me. "I'll buy my own car! From now on I'm on my own! I make my own decisions!" And he left, without having his dinner.

That made me cry. He stayed gone for a week, and then he turned up one evening in time for dinner. I was ecstatic. "Hello Ma," he said. "I've quit school and I'm working for a telephone company. And I've bought a Chrysler. It's nearly new."

I pretended I thought that was all right though of course I didn't. He was making his own decisions.

I had not told Nancy about my decision yet. She was working in Santa Barbara, and would be home for Christmas when I could break the news; so I concentrated on making it a really good one. I had all the cakes made by the end of November, soaking with brandy in the fridge.

Nancy arrived a few days before Christmas. She was not pleased to hear Michael had left school. And when I told her I was going to live in Rome she was horrified. "Mother you can't be serious," she protested. "You can't even speak the language. How can you earn a living? You're too old to be a dropout!"

How conventional children can be! "I'll put the fare for a return ticket in the bank just in case," I promised

"No good trying to make her see sense. I've tried it," Michael said.

So they dropped the subject thinking I'd give up—but I didn't, and as ever my friends bolstered my resolution.

The first was Hank, who came into the studio after one Wednesday class, and announced he had got me a commission to paint a portrait.

"You?" I guessed.

"No, mon cherie," (he always called me that) "A dog."

"But I don't do animals."

"Look, you want money for your trip, don't you?" he said. "And this dog is very furry. He'll be easy to paint. His mistress gave me this photograph so you can just copy it." He showed me a blurred little snapshot. "She's very rich."

"Well get me a better photograph" I began.

"Can't," Hank said. "The dog's dead. Lady wants a momento. Tell you what, though: I've got a magazine with dogs in it, one just like this. She'll never know the difference." So I did it. I copied a picture of the same breed using a magnifying glass to get all the markings right, and she can't have known the difference because she wrote me a lovely letter in spidery writing to say I had really captured the personality of her "Twinkie". I bought Hank a bottle of champagne.

In the very same week I had another commission. A middle-aged woman came to the studio and said she wanted her portrait painted as a present for her husband. She said she was 50 (more like 60, I thought) and wanted to look 45, "So will you paint out some of the wrinkles, not all of them, or people will think I am vain but smooth out the neck, like this," she added, pulling at the skin. "You see, I want to look sexy."

She was in fact a pretty woman, plump with soft grey curls, wide blue eyes and rose-flushed cheeks. She brought a low-cut blue dress with her.

"Oh, dear," I thought ."But I need the money." So I painted her, and adjusted the wrinkles to taste, her husband was happy and I added the fee to my Rome fund.

Step by step I was moving towards my new life, closing down the old, sometimes with sadness and nostalgia. One evening when I was cleaning up after a class, my landlord Forgarty came in to the studio. He stood in his familiar, awkward way, jingling the change in his pocket, and turning his head so that I could not see his tears, he told me Bella had died. I wept too. Everything was changing.

Now I had to start getting rid of the detritus of a lifetime and 24 years of marriage ready for my big adventure, and despite the excitement of a new future I felt the melancholy of severance from the past. What's more it was physically exhausting because a lot of my past seemed to be jammed into the garage. I sat on a box in the middle of it all and, as one does, started reading old letters.

Michael was helping me, unpacking storage cases and throwing stuff out but it was slow going because everything evoked memories. "Hey! Remember frying chicken and potatoes on the beach on this while we fished on the pier with Dad?" Michael shouted over, holding up a huge skillet. "And here's my rod!"

How could I forget those days on the beach, putting the tiddlers he caught in the 'fridge at home and cooking them as if they were some gourmet feast.

"How I miss you, my dearest Nancy", I was reading from a letter my husband sent to me in California when he was in Philadelphia, and with the thought of what was lost and what could have been, I started quietly to cry. Michael came over and took the bundle of letters "I'm going to burn them," he said. "They're part of the past now. You're going to start a new life, Mother. Let's leave this for today and I'll clean out the rest later."

And so the days passed in preparations, art classes, moments of doubt and exultation, as I planned an exhibition for the end of the spring term for the students I hoped to sell my own pictures as well and booked a ticket on the Italian liner, the Cristoforo Colombo because I could take so much more luggage by boat. It was to sail from New York , destination Trieste after 15 days at sea.

Meanwhile Michael got engaged to a pretty girl who was much too young for marriage, then they got disengaged, and he sold his expensive car which used up most of his salary from the telephone company, bought a cheap old banger instead and went back to school. I could see him growing into a responsible adult and felt easier about leaving him.

Time was now passing so fast I decided to end the classes in May instead of June so that I could dismantle the studio and sell the furniture. And it also seemed sensible to pass my driving test because a driving licence can be a useful form of identification abroad. I've never really wanted to drive. In fact, the thought of being in charge of a car terrified me—but not nearly as much as it terrified the driving instructor.

Michael gave me some preliminary lessons and I gathered from the sounds he made that he did not feel secure with me at the wheel. As I moved across lanes to turn right with a truck driver's yell of "Jesus Christ, lady!" ringing in my ears I tried to stay calm and assured Michael that Saint Anthony, my special guardian would look after me. He always had. I would pass the driving test.

Michael made some remarks about St Anthony getting danger money and I should put some extra money in the envelope, "And write, like, 'For Tony from Nancy—thanks in advance' ".

Anyway, I did pass my test though at first the driving examiner said I had failed. So I explained I only wanted to use the licence as identification and was about to leave for Italy to live, so would never drive a car in the USA. "Do you promise that?" he demanded. I showed him the one-way ticket I'd just bought for the Cristoforo Colombo."

"OK" he agreed, and passed me. I kept my word and have never driven a car since.

One by one I was ticking off the tasks to departure date. I bought a huge second-hand trunk from the Good Will shop, filled it so full Michael had to squash down the lid, and sent it off in advance; we finished clearing out the studio, Fogarty came in with some champagne and as we raised our glasses he said he was going to sell up and move as well. My students' last art exhibition turned into a goodbye party, and the Toastmistress Club held a champagne lunch and presented me with a set of luggage.

My exhibition was in June. To my delight Iona and a small group of other friends declared they were going to organise it. Cleora who was a harpist lived in a luxurious villa up in the canyon and her husband Homer had built her a harp-shaped swimming pool in the garden, around which they hung my 54 paintings. For the exhibition they brought in yet more champagne, hired a guest singer and a man to park the cars, and it was a great social success though at first it looked as if I would only sell a few canvases. However by the end of the month every one had gone and I had enough money to feel secure for at least the first few weeks in Rome.

By now I had prepared as thoroughly as I could. The Cristoforo Colombo would dock in Trieste and passengers would be taken by boat to Venice where my travel agent had booked me into a small hotel. The next day I would catch the train to Rome and stay at the Texas Pensione. I had contacted my Congressman and he had written me a letter for the American Counsel General in Rome saying he would appreciate any assistance given to me, and one of my former students, Fanny, who lived in New York and her husband invited me to stay with them for the few days before the ship sailed.

By this time, after so much preparation and champagne, I was ready for adventure. But first Nancy and Michael came to stay in the now almost-empty flat, and we talked and reminisced, conscious that this was the last of our family life together and I asked them to keep a kindly eye on their angry, confused father. A few days later, they waved me off at the Los Angeles airport, full of admonishments to take care, like anxious parents seeing off a teenager.

Now despite the anticipation I felt at peace. Fanny and her husband met me in New York and they held a farewell party at which I met a very attractive widower of my own age, tall, with bright blue eyes—but I was on the move and Adonis himself would not have stopped me now.

I embarked on July 1st. Not without a heart-stopping hitch because I appeared to be missing from the passenger list until they discovered my maiden name, which was the one under which I had been registered.

Waving farewell from the deck of that huge liner and slowly leaving the harbour within sight of the Statue of Liberty I could not help thinking of my forbears on both sides of the family who had arrived at this spot from Italy in the last century, alien and friendless, with their hopes and cherished memories of their old homes. And now I was returning, but as an American, and I felt as if I was following some unextinguished homing instinct.

So the real adventure started.

I had a small cabin to myself, no frills, just the barest comforts for the 15-day journey and I looked forward to the parties, swimming, sophisticated Italian food, making new friends and all the other activities you get on an ocean liner. I did not expect to meet the Mob.

In the dining room we were assigned tables, two or three people to each, and I found myself with Trixi, a whip-slim flamboyant divorcee from Reno. She had black hair and sharp features and was obviously on the prowl. She chatted amiably enough, but if she saw something better, like a man, she was off like a shot. The other diner was Nick, who made a point of being charming to me, which annoyed Trixi.

"He's making a play for you," she hissed to me before he arrived one lunchtime.

"I don't like him. He looks like a gangster and probably married," I hissed back. He was pallid and reminded me a bit of the actor George Raft. He said he ran a "Go Go Topless Club" in San Francisco, so I supposed he stayed indoors too much.

"You're frigid, that's what you are," Trixi said. She was jealous.

By the end of the week I knew most of the other passengers and one day, after I won the fancy hat competition and was awarded a certificate by the captain, a young couple started chatting to me. The husband, John, asked me what I thought of Nick.

"Not much. Something funny about him," I said.

A few days later they invited me to have a drink in their cabin and John told me he was on secret work for the New York District Attorney (his wife Ann was his cover). Then he said he was on the trail of some crooks. Apparently Nick was one of them and there was to be a secret Mafia meeting on board at five o'clock before Nick and his mobster pals joined the others in Palermo.

"We want to know who they are," John said. "They've been pretending not to know each other on the ship, but we know which room they've booked for the meeting. Would you be willing to burst in as if by mistake and take a quick look round and then identify some of them to me after? You seem to know most of the people on the ship. I'd really appreciate your help."

"I'll do it," I said. So just after five o'clock I gate crashed the meeting, stood in the doorway apologising profusely while I counted heads—seven of them—and my portrait-painter's eye memorised their features. I was able later to point them all out to John, who said it was a tremendous help.

Nothing else so exciting happened on the rest of the trip— not even the waiter spilling his crepes flambé on the floor, which sent a tongue of fire shooting down the centre of the dining room, though it caused a bit of excitement among those nearest as they doused it energetically with table cloths and jugs of water.

Every day added to my suntan and my anticipation sharpened as we stopped at Lisbon, Athens, Palermo (good bye to Nick), Naples and Pompeii, which I had missed last time round, and then we were in Trieste. The boat for Venice was waiting: one night at the small hotel, next day the train, and Rome.

When I went through the doors of the Texas Pensione and the trunk containing all my worldly possessions was deposited from the hotel van, I felt dizzy with happiness and excitement at the thought of what was to come.

# Part II

## Life in Rome

# Chapter 27

I sat in the Piazza Navona trying to make one cup of coffee last a long time and watched the sunshine dance and glitter on Bernini's fountain. The drops bounced then met in streams which gushed down figures representing the four great rivers of Europe, Asia, Africa and America, down to a hollowed rock, a lion and horse with flowing manes and a scaly sea serpent while above stretched the long, thin obelisk brought from Egypt by the conquering emperor Domitian.

At each end of the piazza water tumbled from two more ancient fountains; and musicians, a sword-swallower, portrait painters, street traders vied for attention in the carnival atmosphere. It was like this every day. It was noisy and hot, and, I mused as I sat sipping cappuccino at one of the small round tables of Tre Scalini , it was never dull.

More than a week had already passed and I was still staying at the Texas Pensione and wandering down in the early evenings to the Piazza Navona to watch the unending theatre, but now I was starting to worry about the need to find a small apartment to rent. I must get one soon, and a studio as well so that I could start work. My savings would not last forever. Without a word of Italian and not knowing the city, it was turning out to be difficult. Lucky I had banked the money for a return ticket to California, but the thought of going back in defeat made my spirits sink. I took another sip of coffee as a slim, dark-haired woman walked by with a tray looking in vain for an empty table. I gestured to her to share mine and she sat down with a smile.

That was the start of a friendship that has lasted over 35 years.

Rolande was from Belgium and married to an Italian American so she spoke French, fluent Italian, and passable English as well. "I'll help you to find an apartment," she said when I told her of my problem. "I've been living here for years now—in fact my apartment is quite close to the piazza. We'll go through the newspaper adverts then go together to have a look so that I can translate for you."

Next day she called round for me at the pensione and we set out with a list. The first place we visited was tiny. The second was smaller still.

"How about this one? said Rolande translating from a notice pinned to a door: '"For rent. Three rooms." This might do.'

We pushed open a huge door and went from bright sunlight into deep gloom. There was a tiny lighted bulb hanging from a wall, a beaten earth floor and a long, dark passage, at the end of which we could make out the form of a heavily built woman up to her elbows in soapy water and a pile of laundry. Some light filtered down on her from an open window above

"Le stanze?—the rooms?" she repeated. "Si!" And shaking off soap and water, she stuck her head through an open doorway, and yelled, "Salvatore! Salvatore!" In minutes, like a pixie in a pantomime appeared a beautifully dressed dapper little man who smiled affectionately at her as she gave her instructions.

Salvatore beckoned and we followed him up a spiral of marble steps- then up another, and another, and another. Puffing and perspiring we staggered at last through a tall door—and into an elegant room with a beamed ceiling, a fireplace and long, deep-set windows. True, there was a hole in the floor, plaster was falling off the walls, and the whole lot needed painting, but as Salvatore said when he flung open the shutters to reveal a roof-scape of terra cotta tiles and balconies crammed with flowers, "La vista!"—the view—"E magnifico!"

It was—and it seemed our quest was ended. Who cared about a bit of peeling paint? "Where's the kitchen?" asked Rolande. "La cucina?"

Salvatore had opened the shutters of another window to reveal another angle on the view.

"And the kitchen?" Rolande persisted. Eventually with a resigned sigh Salvatore opened a cupboard door and pointed to what looked like a marble horse-trough. "La cucina!" he announced. Rolande and I exchanged astonished glances.

"And the bathroom?"

Salvatore walked on to the balcony which tilted perilously. At the far end was a water closet with a makeshift door he had made himself from scraps of wood. "La gabinetta," he said.

Outside Rolande and I fell laughing into the nearest cafe and fortified ourselves with chocolate. "Imagine trying to cook...the bathroom...the view..." Funny as it was, niggling anxiety occupied my mind.

Two days later I was starting to despair of finding anything, then Rolande rang to say she had seen a "for let" sign in the Via Parione. I already knew the street: it is narrow, dark and crooked and opens into the Piazza Navona. With reignited optimism I hurried over.

"Here it is." Rolande stopped before two massive, heavily carved doors standing slightly ajar. We squeezed through and found ourselves in bright sunlight in a circular cobbled courtyard and looked up to a building swathed in wisteria. It was like cracking open a stone and finding coloured crystals inside.

A porter greeted us and went to find "la Contessa", the owner of the property. When she came she was just as a contessa should be: stately, elegant and charming.

"A young man rented the apartment for two years," she explained as we went up in a lift to the fourth floor. "He furnished it and paid six months in advance, then he just vanished. I haven't seen him since."

We were in a large room with a high ceiling and two big windows deeply recessed into thick, 400-year-old walls. Through the open casements I looked across a swathe of the city, a jumble of tiled roofs and red geraniums in the foreground fading to a pale blue horizon. A soft breeze fluttered the curtains and threw shadows across white walls, bookshelves, two single beds, a chest on which stood a small bust of John Kennedy and some pretty antique furniture.

The bathroom had blue tiles and opened to a balcony, and there was a tiny kitchen that contained all the essential things. I loved it at once and paid three months rent in advance.

The contessa said that as the furniture belonged to the young man who had disappeared, she had better store it for him. It was very mysterious, she said, his vanishing. But she had kept the place empty for him and she could not do that forever. If I signed an inventory I could perhaps borrow some of the antiques. I did. Then Rolande and I set about getting furniture from the flea market.

We found two divan beds that would look like sofas in the daytime and covered them with ochre spreads and autumn-coloured cushions. I bought a chest with a marble top and another marble slab to put on a low, rather battered table Rolande gave me, a pair of antique lamps, six chairs specially made in the cane shop across the road and hung some pictures on the walls. It was looking pretty good and it felt like home.

For the next 20 years it was my refuge, a venue for parties, a Roman haven for guests and a constant source of delight. I never tired of looking out of those rooftop windows, walking across the quiet cobbled courtyard, through the magnificent carved doors and into the narrow street alive with cafes, voices and street traders.

A few days after settling in I went out to buy vegetables. It was high summer and hot, but the buildings threw cooling shade across the road as I walked carefully over the cobbles. There were pushcarts laden with fruit and vegetables picked that morning, red and yellow peppers, tomatoes, fresh basil, roughly woven baskets spilling out bunches of black and green grapes and the air held the scent of earth and fruit and flowers. I needed some salt. "Ah, si, Signora; salt is from the tobacconist. And postage stamps? Also from the tobacconist." Across the road I saw "la Polleria"—the chicken shop where I could buy new laid eggs and I stepped off the pavement.

Too intent, I did not see the little red Fiat 500 careering down the road. The driver reacted fast, stopped dead, but not before he had pinned my foot under his front wheel on the passenger side.

He thought he had just missed me and sat back with a resigned silly-woman-now-move-will-you expression on his face.

Standing with one's foot under the wheel of a car is not entirely comfortable and the trouble is, the driver does not feel a thing. So when I tried to communicate that I could not move by jabbing my finger downward at my foot and showing an agonised expression, he merely got annoyed. Apparently that particular gesture is Italian for "I'm damn well not moving an inch and you can do your worst."

He started honking his horn and shouting at me. An old woman dressed in black ran over, saw my foot under the wheel and started hitting him with her purse. Italians love a good noise so there was soon a little crowd yelling at the driver who carried on sitting there and shouting back. The man from the news-stand came over and gave me a wooden fruit box to sit on, and started fanning my face with a newspaper. I was not in much pain because my foot had gone numb, but by now everyone was shouting at the driver, and he finally got the message.

He got out of the car and saw why I could not move. He put his hand over his mouth, shut his eyes, opened them and rolled them skyward, slapped his forehead—all of which I presumed was Italian for "Santa Maria! What have I done!" Then he moved his car off my foot, which promptly ballooned to treble its size.

Two men wanted to take me to hospital, still cursing the driver as they supported me under each arm. I gingerly tried out my foot. It was not broken. I would go home. As they led me gently away I caught a last glimpse of the driver. He was leaning over the steering wheel with his hands over his head, a picture of dejection as the spectators yelled more abuse at him. I felt as if I had taken part in one of Fellini's films.

When we reached the door to my courtyard I thanked my escorts and turned to leave them. Not quite fast enough: one who had tucked his hand under my arm gave my breast a quick squeeze as he withdrew it. I turned and glared at him. He grinned back and shrugged and walked away with his friend, both laughing.

# Chapter 28

For the first few days in my new apartment I just soaked in the pleasure of living. Never, on that first visit to Rome, which now seemed so far away, could I have dreamt of homing up in a mediaeval building beside the most beautiful of all the piazzas.

I adapted to the Italian rhythms: rising early in the mornings, taking a leisurely lunch at one o'clock followed by the sacred siesta, for which everything shuts down until five then opens again to life at full blast till midnight. But my sense of peace did not last long. My savings were draining away.

How could I stay unless I found work, and found it quickly? And for that I needed a studio. It would have to be central, near public transport and with parking space, an elevator, toilet facilities, central heating, good lighting .

Rolande and I pored over adverts. It had been difficult enough finding an apartment, but this was impossible. By now it was August, hot and humid. I had started waking up early in the mornings in a sweat of anxiety dreading another day of fruitless searching; dreading even more having to give up.

In the freshness of the morning before the heat grew too fierce I'd go to the Tre Scalini in the piazza for a cappuccino and brioche as I read the "for rent" adverts in the Daily American. The newspaper has a Today in Rome column, and on this particular day an item caught my eye: the Artists' Students League was meeting at 7pm in St Paul's Protestant church. I knew where that was. I decided to go.

By this time my sprits were so low I went into the great baroque church of St Agnese on the Piazza Navona and in tears, begged God for help. What else could I do? I would take two more weeks, and if I could find nothing by then, surely it was a sign to go home.

In the evening, I took the bus to the Artists' meeting . When I got to St Paul's Church it seemed to be in darkness and I could not find an entrance. After a few minutes, two women arrived and went to a little recessed door, which I had not noticed so I hurried after them.

"Are you going to the meeting? Could I join you?".

They turned to me. "Of course". They sounded friendly and they had reassuring American voices.

We went from the courtyard into a small room where there were about 15 people, a few British and Australians, but mainly Americans sitting around and chatting and they welcomed me into their circle. I saw no sign of artists' materials, and nobody was talking about art which was surprising, but when a cadaverous man called Harvey asked me what I was doing in Rome, I told him all about my plans to open an art school and filled him in about my successful studio in California.

"Oh, painting! Now that's something I always wanted to do!" said a tall blonde called Lucy. She was wearing lots of jangly gold jewellery and said she came to Rome every year to buy Gucci for her boutique in Florida.

"And tell me, my dear," said a quavering voice at my elbow. "How long have you been at it?" The speaker was a middle aged woman with untidy grey hair, and her pale eyes widened with distress when I replied, "About thirty years."

"Oh, how dreadful!" she gasped. All eyes seemed to turn on me with sympathy.

Something was wrong. "Excuse me," I mumbled, "You are the Artists' Students League?" My voice faded off as I saw the astounded faces around me.

Someone said, "This is an A.A. meeting. Alcoholics Anonymous."

I started laughing. "And I can get drunk on the smell of a cork."

"So can we," a voice broke in and all around reformed drunks taking one day at a time were laughing too.

"I thought you were an Artists' Association!"

"We thought you were trying to get off the bottle!"

"And all I wanted was to find a room for a studio."

"Ask Pastor Whitcomb. Perhaps he'll let you borrow this one."

So I asked Pastor Whitcomb who said it was impossible, while managing to sound so regretful that as I caught the bus home chalking up another defeat, I couldn't help feeling more cheerful.

Tomorrow, as Scarlet O'Hara said, was another day.

Tomorrow though, was the 15th of August, the start of Ferragosto, which means the fading of summer, when Romans leave the city for their vacenze and the shops shut and you might as well go home.

It saw me again sitting in the Tre Scalini with a morning cappuccino, scanning the Daily American, the ads. page, the social column—and to my surprise I saw the Toastmasters' Club was meeting for lunch at the YMCA. The Toastmistresses had been my lifeline in California. It was where I learned to speak on my feet, made friends, started my painting studio, recruited my first students. Perhaps the same mixture would work again. I rang the YMCA.

Giovanni Cassale the director answered.

"I've been a Toastmistress in California for 18 years," I began, "and I've just come to live in Rome, and I wondered if I could, well, go to the Toastmasters' meeting."

Giovanni Cassale sounded pleased. Would I be their guest at lunch? Would I give a short talk about what I was doing? he asked. So I dressed up and turned up and found myself the only woman among 20 men who applauded with enthusiasm and said that, as a matter of fact, they wouldn't mind learning how to paint, and the American advisor on the YMCA staff, Ed Carlson offered afterwards to show me round the building, which was the usual sort of thing: partly a cheap hotel, partly a meeting place with some sports facilities, a canteen-style restaurant, a coffee bar and a drinks bar. Ed Carlson said it was the only YMCA in the world where you could buy alcohol.

We reached the third floor and went into a big room with windows on three sides. Like the others it was featureless, unfurnished, with some junk lying around. But when I said goodbye, I left feeling I had met some potential students to add to the alcoholic ladies if only I could find the right studio.

That night, I lay in bed and thought about the big, empty room. I couldn't get it out of my mind. It would, after all, be ideal. It had everything, even a coffee bar in the building and parking underneath. I could hardly wait for dawn.

Next morning I rang Ed Carlson, who said to try the Head of Sports and Social Affairs. At the YMCA, Ed introduced me to a long, thin man, and together we went up to the room. It really did look forlorn and scruffy, but to me it was palatial.

"You see?" said the Head of Sports. "Not much good, is it?"

"But it's wonderful," I enthused.

"What could you use it for?"

I explained.

"Oh, we've had that sort of class before. Never works. They all leave. Look at all this stuff : it's the remains of the last one. Well, if you really think you can run an art class here, I won't charge you rent, but you can pay a percentage on each student instead. How's that?"

How was it! If I could have reached I'd have kissed him. In my mind, I saw the dusty room cleaned, furnished, smart, full of people, a reception with wine and food and waiters. It would hold ten students easily. That meant eleven easels, eleven stools and—well I had better start.

The first step was to make sure all the right people heard about this great new contribution to art tuition in Rome. I started drawing up a list. The ladies from Alcoholics Anonymous. Toastmasters. And, um... the trouble was, I didn't know anyone else yet. But luckily the pretty woman called Amanda who lived in a flat above mine worked at the American embassy and she said she would get me a list from her office.

Meanwhile I contacted the American Women's Club of Rome at their Hilton Hotel office—they had 300 members, most of whom had husbands in various big companies—and Amanda came up with names of ambassadors, consul generals and other people on the embassy social round.

I picked names from them at random and wrote out the invitation: "The Sunday Painters of Rome and Nancy Kominsky Request the Pleasure of the Company of...etc. Then I dashed to the printer's and ordered 300 engraved invitations.

Now I felt at the point of no return.

No more sitting in the Piazza Navona drinking coffee: I had to clean the room and furnish it, order paints, drinks, canapes, canvases...

Not quite every business had closed for August, which was lucky because I was able to find a little art shop in the maze of back streets, and the owner was glad to do some trade.

He was a gentle, courteous man, and his niece Maria who had the same ways spoke English so I was able to explain to her what I needed. First, that easel in the window. It was just the thing. Could she get eleven?

To be sure they could: uncle would order them straight away, this minute.

"And these paints?" I explained they had to be the exact colours because of my teaching method: quarter teaspoon of titanium white, half a teaspoon of yellow ochre... Maria's eyes danced. "What if we supply kits?" she said. "All the right colours, with brushes, and the canvases?"

So we did a deal with 20 per cent off. Maria's uncle sent her out to get coffee and glasses of sambuca to celebrate. And within a few months there was even more reason to raise a glass because by then I had 55 students.

Just as everything had gone wrong the weeks before, now everything started to go right. I found a shop near the piazza where a man made me eleven stools with rush seats; and a department store where I bought eleven folding trays, big enough to hold a palette and tubes of paint. The easels arrived, and the invitations were sent out; I booked a couple of waiters, ordered wine and food and put some of my pictures on the walls. There was to be no second chance. As I'd done once in California, I was going for broke.

Just a week before the opening I began to feel jittery. Had I done enough? What I needed was some publicity. Amanda suggested contacting Pat McNally, who wrote Lend Me Your Ears in the Daily American so I rang Mr McNally next day.

He invited me to his office, but as it was on the fringe of the city, I asked him if he could come to my flat instead. When he arrived I started telling him about the studio.

He looked perplexed. "Aren't you from the Getty Oil Exploration Company? I thought... I'd been expecting..." He started to laugh. "I think you want my wife—she's Pat McNally. I'm Jim. As a matter of fact I wouldn't mind learning how to paint."

A few days later, the real Pat McNally wrote up the studio in the Daily American. And before the doors opened, the YMCA Head of Sport came up to inspect the room he had last seen empty and abandoned. Now there were red, white and blue flowers in a soup tureen, John Kennedy's bust on a table, my pictures around the walls and waiters stood by with wine and canapés for the first guests.

The grand opening turned out to be a sparkling, noisy, happy party. "Oh! I am so emotion!" declared Rolande, looking French and chic in black crepe. I wore a long, off-the-shoulder pink linen dress with a deep border of woven flowers in different colours, and golden-haired Amanda signed on 22 students.

By the end of the evening, we knew that the Sunday Painters of Rome was no longer a dream. It had arrived.

# Chapter 29

It took a week to organise the studio and classes for 30 students. I wrote to each aspiring painter telling them what equipment to buy, then we settled on three sessions a week, ten to each class. This meant I worked on Monday, Tuesday and Wednesday mornings, 10 am to 1pm—but this was only the start.

Now instead of fearing the future, I awoke daily with a zest for life that belied my middle age, went out to the market, bought fresh bread and fruit, caught the bus to work and felt that at last I belonged in the streets of Rome. With the enthusiasm of a teenager I looked forward to making new friends and exploring the city, free at last from life-long constraints and worries.

At the first lesson I drew a grid on the picture of a bowl of marigolds and showed my students how to mix the colours. Chatter subsided as everyone concentrated and I went round the group who were mainly wives of embassy staff—though there was one brave man called Hans, and one Franciscan nun called Sister Esmeralda on a sabbatical from her convent in California.

Sister Esmeralda wore the black habit and wimple of her order as she slashed on bright colours with the palette knife, her round, jolly face expressing the delight of a pupil being allowed to indulge in a favourite game. "I've always wanted to learn to paint with a knife," she said, layering on the pigment. She was only able to stay a few months before being summoned back to the convent. But the number of other students grew, soon more men as well as women, and I had to expand to evening classes, 7.30 to 10.30pm from Monday to Thursday to accommodate those who had to come after work.

It was hard work and sometimes I felt nauseous and headachy from the constant smell of turpentine and linseed oil. On those days I would be glad to go home and lie down after a salad or a bowl of pasta and a glass of red wine.

One evening when I had asked my neighbour, Amanda to join me for dinner, the telephone rang and it was Beatrice, one of my American students married to a Swiss diplomat. She was frantic, expecting guests to arrive any minute, and the maid had cooked the meat balls till they were a revolting-looking grey.

"Have you got food colouring?" I asked. "Red and green and just a drop of yellow? That should make quite a rich brown. Try mixing it into the meat,"

There was a shout of relief down the line. "It's worked. They look delicious!" Diplomatic embarrassment was avoided and my reputation as a colourful cook established.

Before the year was out I was feeling more settled in Italy than I had felt anywhere before and already through my work and the many embassy parties I had lots of friends, men and women.

There is no country like Italy for raising the morale of a single woman. I do not know the ratio of unmarried men to women in this jewel of the Mediterranean, but it seems to be vastly higher than that of any other country I have visited. One of the more persistent Romeos I encountered was Enrico, an academic with a brother in the government and a matriarchal Mama.

"No Enrico," I said for the hundredth time like a teenager.

"But I'm man and you woman!" he expostulated, a line delivered with such indignation I had to laugh. But I had no wish to lose my new freedom, for each day was worry-free and filled with incident and new interests.

The classes were always fun. If they were not I would have lost my students because they weren't there to suffer for art. We painted still lifes and landscapes, and Hans nagged, only half in joke, to paint a nude.

"You're not good enough for that yet," I told him.

"If we had a live model" he protested

"You can start with copying a marble bust."

I was interrupted by frantic banging at the door and Gina, a pretty brunette who took the men's aerobics class in the gym next door burst in clasping a robe around her curvy body. "Hide me!" she gasped. "The carabinieri are after me!" She looked around like a scared rabbit but there was no place to conceal her, not even a cupboard. I had an idea.

"Take off your robe and stand with your back to the door. Hold this vase on your shoulder." Turning to the class (by now it included four men) I hissed, "Get painting!"

A few minutes later there was a knock on the door, and two carabinieri were there. "This is a life class", I said indignantly, only half opening the door. One of them glanced in. "Scusi!" he said and withdrew quickly.

When they had gone Gina quickly put on her robe. "Carlo in reception, he send them up by the wrong stairs and phone to tell me," she said. "I go now." Next day I heard the rest of the story from a furious director of the YMCA.

Gina's "aerobic" lessons were not the conventional kind. Carlo had been supplying her with clients and taking a cut.

After the morning painting lesson I often lunched with friends from the class. Helen, a Jordanian who by mistake had eaten some of the still life I had chosen with meticulous care at the fruit market took me by way of apology, to a pretty pizzeria tucked away in a little square, where we met Fellini. I had once read the film director's cards at a party when I told him he should get rid of some of his hangers-on, and he said he had followed my advice. I met one of the hangers-on some weeks after, looking unfriendly.

Later in the week I lunched with three other friends, including Mary whose husband worked at the UN Food and Agriculture Office (FAO) in Rome. He was one of their fish experts. Mary, nearly in her sixties, was distressed and nervous as she told us that they were being posted to Kenya.

We were at Francesco's where the speciality was a seafood pasta dish cooked in a paper bag. The waiter took our order and we sipped vino bianco as Mary, near to tears, continued, "I don't want to go. If only I could carry on with my painting here."

She had joined the class to "get out of herself" after her 23-year-old son was killed in a road accident. At first she had been quiet and withdrawn, but gradually she made friends and became seriously interested in painting.

"You can carry on in Kenya," I said "You've learned enough now."

"But I can't remember how to mix the colours," she said.

One of the others chimed in, "I can't either. That's why I write them down. Nancy, why don't you do a manual? Write out all the formulae like a dictionary of colour and we could photocopy them."

It had crossed my mind before, but I was daunted by all the work involved. What clinched it was Mary's husband, Harry, a tall out-doors man calling me to say how much the painting classes had helped Mary.

"Before John was killed she used to be so strong," he said, "and we've been in some pretty hairy places. She's been charged by elephants, and when she was expecting our daughter, she had to row across a swollen river to get to the hospital. Nothing seemed to daunt her. Now she needs some help"

It took me a long time but I wrote out the guide to colour-mixing, had the sheets copied and handed them out to the class. Mary later wrote from Kenya sounding cheerful and saying she was getting on well with her painting.

That, I suppose would have been the end of my literary efforts had I not met "the girls"—two tall American ladies in their sixties, with gloves and pearls and lively minds. One, Eve Learner, was the widow of a New York copyright attorney and she had been Dean of Radcliff College.

When I told her about the colour guide she said, "You must turn it into a proper book. Get it published."

Like many a complete novice, I thought, "Right, I'll do it. That shouldn't be too difficult."

It did not take me long to realise it was. My attention flagged. I rambled into a muddle. Then I decided to write it like a cookery book.

1.   Select materials
2.   Arrange workspace.
3.   Do the drawing
4.   Mix and shade colours following exact measurements
5.   Apply paint

That was the beginning. Next came four subject categories. Floral, fruit, landscapes and seascapes.

Without frequent urging by Eve perhaps I would have given up. Between teaching and my social life there was not much time for being an author. And there was an added complication.

To my delight, at the beginning of September, I had a letter from my daughter Nancy, now in her late twenties, saying she was going to come to stay for a few weeks. She had left her job with the Los Angeles bank and an ex-boyfriend, and felt like a change. My flat was small—too small, though there were two divan beds—but I had missed the family more than I realised and hoped Nancy would be charmed by the big fireplace, rooftop views, and the old buildings.

It was a lovely day in October when she arrived. In no time, like me, she loved the city, though the constant attention of men in the streets irked her. One day we were caught in a frightening anti-American demonstration over the Vietnamese War. It turned into a battle between the crowd and police with batons, and we had to be rescued by an Italian in the newspaper kiosk, who grabbed us, pushed us into the hut and pulled down the shutters.

Although she liked my 400-year-old flat, one or two features about it bothered Nancy. She thought it inconvenient having to use the hammer to unlock the bathroom door, and to open the kitchen window. Then the way the rain came in, depending on the direction of the wind , and my washing the linen in the bath using an old scrub-board, and leaning out over the balcony to dry things on a wire stretched from the next building .To her it all seemed just too quaint for comfort.

On my side I was not sure that Rome was the right place for an American girl of dating age, but Christmas was coming, the Piazza Navona was filled with decorated stalls and lights and nativity scenes and music. I closed the studio for a month, and together we enjoyed some sightseeing.

Before the Christmas holiday began my friend at the American Consulate rang to say they needed an American girl to help out for a few weeks at the American United Services Organisation because one of their staff was ill. She wondered whether my daughter would do it. It was a paid job, near the Vatican and it involved meeting American servicemen and their families over the festive period. Nancy was glad to earn some pocket money and enjoyed being there. Within days, she was going out with a young Air Force officer on leave from Saudi Arabia.

He called around one evening and I opened the door to a sandy-haired six-footer, about 30 years old with an engaging grin, whom I liked immediately. He introduced himself as Larry Benson, from San Francisco.

I was not surprised when, in February, they decided to get married. I had never seen Nancy happier. Larry bought her an engagement ring in the Piazza Navona and the jeweller took them both out to lunch, then we had an engagement party and they left for California together. I went over briefly for their wedding in June and left feeling happy that she was secure and had someone to care for her.

Back in Rome, I had to get down to some serious work on the book. "Keep it simple," I kept telling myself, as I wrote and re-wrote.

By the time I reopened the classes in September, the words were finished though I still had to do the explanatory drawings, and the colour work, and that took me another two months. Now I had to look for publishers.

I had decided to spend Christmas in Philadelphia staying with my eldest sister Marie and visiting my mother who was now a permanent resident in Norristown Hospital. With all the optimism and total ignorance of a novice I thought I might as well take my book around to some publishers in New York while I was there.

One of my students, Cleo thought it was a good idea because the editor-in-chief of Doubleday was a close friend of hers and she said she would write to him and ask him to see me in December. Another friend knew an editor at Lippincott, a publisher in Philadelphia, and as I was going to be there anyway, it seemed an obvious call to make.

Eve, who had started me off on the book project, said it was best to get an agent and wrote down the name of a woman in New York, adding that she probably wouldn't take me but it was worth a try.

When I got there I checked into a small hotel and rang the agent. "I don't take unpublished writers," she said.

I told her I had got some appointments lined up.

"Well, if you can get them to see you before Christmas, " she said, "Tell them Lucille Rosen's your agent, and call me back afterwards."

I went to Doubleday, met Cleo's friend, the editor who gave me some helpful criticism. I'd mixed too much story telling in with the art information. Make it one thing or the other, he said, and in any case, he added kindly, his company did not handle that sort of book.

Afterwards I met Lucille Rosen, who went through the manuscript, crossing out pages and paragraphs with her gold pencil. She told me to re-write it and send it on to her and then she would send me a contract to sign.

"That," I thought, "is one big step forward. Now I have an agent." And looking through the butchered manuscript, I could see that she was right about the changes.

Snow was falling in New York and the streets were decked for Christmas as I checked out of my dingy hotel and caught the train for Philadelphia where my sister Maria was waiting for me.

Next day I went to see the editor at Lippencott whose response to my manuscript was predictable. This teaching method, he said, would stifle creativity. I reported back to my agent. "I thought they'd say that," she said.

As soon as we could Maria and I went to Norristown Hospital to see mother. I knew the elegant and accomplished woman of my childhood had gone for ever, but now she seemed to have shrivelled into a pathetic figure, lost and mystified by visitors whom she saw as strangers. I held back tears as we handed her small gifts, which she received with childlike delight. When she remembered who I was, she chatted amiably and seemed rational, but Maria visited regularly and said that when she had taken her home the moods changed quickly. I left with sadness though knowing that she was well cared for and apparently contented. .

A white Christmas came and went as we celebrated within the warmth and comfort of Marie's family home. But now I felt out of place in the city of my childhood. I longed to go home to Rome and in January I flew back out.

The next few months, when I was not teaching, I was re-writing my book. Out went all the trivia, anything that distracted from the main teaching theme. I sent the copy to my agent and after some weeks the rejection slips started to come in. It was "too much like other books," "too expensive because of the colour" and so on. "I thought that would happen," said the agent.

I was disappointed.

"Well let's publish it ourselves," one of the students suggested. She was Heidi Klaus from Munich, worked at FAO, and she knew someone who had a little printing business in Switzerland. He designed and printed art books. We could ask him.

The printer sounded doubtful, then he read the manuscript and cheered up. He said he thought it would sell. He'd have a go.

It became his obsession as he photographed the spoons for measuring, the tubes of paint, made me re-do colour charts and diagrams, cajoled his assistant, and at length, at a cost of $1,500, produced a thousand books on heavy glossy paper with a spiral binding and a photograph of me teaching the class on the back.

We were ecstatic. But when I wrote to my agent and sent her a copy she was furious. It was "vanity publishing"—the crime of the amateur, and now no respectable professional would look at it.

Just weeks later I had another letter. A respectable publisher—Bobs Merril in New York and the first who had seen it had snapped it up. And there was an advance cheque in the envelope which more than paid my "vanity" debts.

I had to go back to New York to speak to the publishers who wanted some small changes, did away with the spiral binding, put a picture of red apples on the cover and discussed promotion in the press and TV. It had a lot of publicity and in June 1970 I had to go to the US to do some promotions, travelling around the country.

It was success beyond my expectations and I should have been full of energy, but I wasn't. I felt ill. Just when so many gates were opening. I went to a doctor who diagnosed angina and advised me not to work for a year.

# Chapter 30

The thought of not working for a year just when everything was getting interesting was too much to bear and I had every intention of watering down the doctor's advice to just taking things a little more slowly. Cut out some of the parties, perhaps. Level out the social life. But on the aircraft home I had to be given oxygen, and was taken off on a stretcher, so something had to change.

Yet how could I not work for a year? What would I live on?

It is my everlasting good fortune that I make friends easily—the one blessing I seem to have inherited from my father—and now with unstinting generosity they came to my aid.

One bought some of my paintings, paying me lavishly, which helped to cover the rent of my flat. Another, the American consul Tony Gentile, whose wife Eve was one of my students produced, like a magician, the ideal person to run my studio for a year. They had a friend from their hometown Ohio staying with them. His name was Joe de Cosmo, a graphic artist in his forties who had taken a year off and was looking around for a way of keeping himself in Rome. I liked him and he agreed right away to look after the studio until I could work again. We decided to split the proceeds and as it was still the Christmas holiday I had time to show him my teaching method.

The arrangement worked well. He enjoyed the work, was able to rent a small flat, and the students liked him.

Meanwhile my health deteriorated. Some days I could hardly walk, a lump appeared under my left ear and my voice was often hoarse.

I went to a doctor who could not see anything in the X-rays. So I flew to Philadelphia and stayed with my sister Marie while I went to a specialist there.

The specialist said I had a tumour—he could not tell yet whether it was malignant or not, but they would have to cut it out. This would also mean cutting facial nerves, which would disfigure me because that would make half my face droop.

Feeling insecure and unsure, I flew to Burbank to see my former doctor, and he referred me to the local hospital where there happened to be a panel meeting on tumours. .

Three specialists examined me and made the same diagnoses as the doctor in Philadelphia. There had to be surgery. I told my doctor I was worried about the cost, and he admitted me to the City of Hope National Cancer Hospital, which was free to those unable to pay. (When eventually I made some money I sent a donation.)

The surgeon who was going to do the job was the split of John Wayne.

Six foot tall, he was dressed like a cowboy in boots, a check shirt, a neckerchief clasped with a pair of brass steers and a Stetson which he raised from his head on entering the ward. He had a long, shambling walk. "Howdy!" he cried. "How y'all? We'll have ya right in no time!"

I thought, "I hope you're right."

They shaved the hair from the left side of my head, and another doctor asked if they could televise the operation. "OK doc. Just do the best you can," I said. It was my first appearance on the screen and I wasn't expecting to enjoy it.

After the operation, in intensive care with my neck swathed in bandages, two doctors came in with the surgeon. "Blink your eyes," the John Wayne character said.

I blinked. "Now smile." I smiled.

The doctors clapped. "We've saved your facial nerves," said John Wayne. "The tumour was causing your angina, and it wasn't cancer."

I could have cheered but my voice had gone weak.

Within days I was flying back to Rome. Joe stayed on until there was another wave of anti-Americanism in Rome, when some businesses closed and a number of Americans, including Joe went home. But he had saved the studio for me.

My book was already selling well thanks to the huge amount of publicity it received in the US, which included a double column in the Wall Street Journal, and I contemplated writing another about my teaching method. Student figures were up to 55, many of them had become my friends and I was enjoying a happy combination of work and social events. I reflected that I had come a long way since my friends at the Toastmistress Club first put me on the road. Now new friends in Rome were to take me on to my next life-changing step.

It began with meeting a fellow-guest at a cocktail party given by one of my students. Ned Barnett who was an exporter and his wife Joan, gave famously glamorous parties. This one was in a palazzo near Piazza Venezia.

The apartment had high ceilings, a great stone fireplace and tall windows overlooking a courtyard with Roman figures in it and a fountain and little shrubs.

The aristocracy of Roman government, arts and business society were there, and so was Eduardo Antonelli, a jovial thick-set Italian with his lively wife Gina, both old friends of Ned's. Eduardo was an agent who sold television properties. He spoke good English, a result of being taken prisoner of war by the British in the North Africa campaign and held by them for three years behind barbed wire.

"I've been looking at Ned's paintings," he said over our cocktails and canapés. "Not bad. Says you taught him. Ever thought of making a television programme?"

I told him I'd been on local television in California.

"Gina and I are going to the Monte Carlo Film and Television Festival in April. You ought to come. It's in Cannes."

I needed no persuasion. I closed the studio for a week and went.

A curious thing happened the night before I left. I dreamt that my friend Shirley came into my room and said, "Nancy, you've got a telegram." It wouldn't have been the first time I dreamt something that came true, so I rang her up and gave her my hotel telephone number just in case.

When we reached Cannes, I was at once captivated by the raw excitement and buzz of the festival, the hustling of ambitious men and glamorous women pushing to be noticed, beautiful, brittle, and brash. There were spring flowers everywhere, wine sparkling in glasses, cameras flashing, and along the white festival building just across the road from the dark blue sea, flags of all represented nations were fluttering.

Everyone seemed to be in a rush, making appointments, networking, posing for photographs. Eduardo was an old hand and he had had my name and the title of my book added to the brochures and lists at the booths. Gina and I wandered around while he did his business.

The night before we were due to leave, I had the telegram. It was from Marie saying our mother was not expected to live, and I should fly out immediately to Philadelphia. I did, and by the time I had got there mother had rallied. She lived another 30 years.

It was two years before I returned to Cannes, again with Eduardo, and this time something did happen, which changed my life. I asked an Italian friend, a recent widow called Gabriella to come with me. I thought it would do her good to get away and she was young and elegant and interesting company. Eduardo, as before, introduced me to numerous people then went off to look after his business.

Gabriella and I sat at a table with a glass of Campari and soda each and I looked at the menu. Gabriella was looking over my shoulder at a poster on the wall.

Two English men were looking at it as well. It was one of those old wartime posters familiar in Britain in the early forties, of a couple of women gossiping together on a red bus and behind them, Goering and Hitler are sitting, listening in. There is a warning underneath: "Careless talk costs lives."

"I like to get one of those posters," Gabriella said. "My Enzo like posters."

"I'll see if we can have one," I said, and went to speak to the men.

One of them was thin and bearded and looked at me suspiciously. The other was the opposite: a kind, open face and a ready smile. "Could you tell me where I could get one of those?" I asked the friendly one.

"In the British booth. It's from the TV World At War series," he said.

"I've got a pass for that booth. Do you think they'd give me one?"

"Yes. But what are you doing here? Buying or selling films?"

I told him my idea for the TV programme to teach painting. I had some of my material so I showed it to him.

"Sounds interesting," he said. "My wife's learning to paint and it costs me the earth. Then she goes and hangs her pictures in a cupboard. I think this idea of yours would make a good series. Look, let me borrow the material to show someone I know who might be interested. My name's Fred Buckley, by the way: I represent a film processing company. Ring you at six this evening."

It was a bit of a risk, but I trusted him. And promptly at six, he rang to say he'd made me an appointment next day with Peter Orton, promoter of a number of successful TV programmes including The Muppets. I was almost too excited to sleep that night.

Next morning, I dressed up in my best black trouser suit, with a hat, which I fancied looked rather dashing, and Eduardo took me around to the meeting place. "Tell him I'm your agent," he said as he left.

Fred Buckley was waiting with a tall young man in his thirties, whom he introduced as Peter Orton. Mr Orton nodded and glanced around a trifle impatiently. I explained my project, why it would be perfect for television, how it could tie in with an art company to sponsor painting kits. He started to show more interest.

"Would it do for children?"

"It would do for anyone. Children, retired people, housewives. And I could do a book to go with it."

He made up his mind quickly. "I'll take it. Ask your agent to call me here tomorrow."

Eduardo, Gabriella and I celebrated excitedly with lunch together and Gabriella suggested going to the casino in Monte Carlo to celebrate even more.

"I don't gamble," I said feeling game for anything, "but I'll go to look." And it was worth it. A gallery of characters Toulouse Lautrec would have rejoiced in: an old woman with bleached hair extravagantly swirled around her head, and breasts so large they lay on the table with four ropes of pearls nestling on top of them. She surveyed the table through a jewelled lorgnette and moved the chips with fingers heavy with rings.

Beside her was the most elegant man I have ever seen, fortyish, blond, perfectly groomed in dinner jacket and a white silk shirt revealing a flash of diamond cufflinks as he put down a pile of chips. He moved with languid grace, despite a bunch of small flowers he had tucked into the top pocket of his jacket.

Green that I was, I started sketching. Suddenly there was a large man on both sides of me grabbing an arm each.

"Come with us," one of them said.

"Why?" I protested.

By this time we had crossed the room and were facing an apparently blank wall, then like Mr Big's lackey in a Bond film, the talkative one pressed a button and a door opened. In the room beyond, sitting at a very ornately carved desk sat the Boss.

"Who sent you here?" he snapped.

"No one."

"I'll ask you again: who sent you?" He was getting waspish fast. And (holding out a hand) " I'll take those."

I let him have the sketches. "I'm an artist. I teach art in Rome" I said, mustering some indignation to hide my fright.

"We don't have photographers here," he said, "nor spies taking notes of people who don't want to be noticed. He looked at the pictures. The hint of a smile twitched a lip and his voice un-snapped. "You can go. Don't do any more."

I went back through the hidden door into the gaming room followed by one of the men, who trailed me for the rest of the evening. At every turn he was my shadow. And he waited for me outside the loo. Gabriella, none the richer for the night, thought it was funny.

Back in Rome I awaited the call from Peter Orton. It came in the shape of a letter a month later telling me to go to Montreux in Switzerland where there was a trade fair of recording and video equipment, to do the pilot film.

It would take two days. The man making it was busy selling and demonstrating equipment and I felt the film was a very hurried affair, with me painting a quick picture and ad-libbing to the camera. I thought, "Well that will put them off." But Peter Orton wrote that it would be all right after a bit of editing and he enclosed the contract.

"We're going to make a lot of money," he said encouragingly. It sounded like the right line in positive thinking but when he tried to place it, a couple of TV companies turned it down. Then Harlech Television in Bristol said they would do a series and I could hardly believe it. It was all actually happening. " What shall we call it?" they said. "How about, 'Paint Along With Nancy'?"

# Chapter 31

CONFIRM YOUR FEATURING IN TV SERIES TO BE PRODUCED HERE JANUARY STOP PLEASE ARRANGE FLY TO LONDON SUNDAY NOVEMBER 25$^{TH}$ STOP A TICKET WILL BE PURCHASED IN YOUR NAME BEA LONDON REGARDS ORTON

The telegram was date-stamped 12 November 1973 and followed by advice to pack for a long stay in London. The agent Peter Orton had not been idle: he had lined up contacts, promotion tours, deals, and a book for me to do. This was to be months of concentrated work: enjoyable, but very busy.

HTV would be making a series of 13 programmes, each lasting 26 minutes. In every programme I had to paint a complete picture on screen, explaining what I was doing as I went along, giving viewers tips on how to get the drawing right, mix the paints for colour and tonal values, demonstrating how to use the palette knife, and, of course, it had to be entertaining.

I had been doing the same in the painting classes in Rome so that part did not worry me, but the performance was just a small part of the total work.

"Bring some of your paintings with you," Peter Orton told me. "We can display them on the set." We both knew the importance of capturing the viewers' interest right from the start by showing examples of what they would be able to do themselves, so I packed a few of my favourite pictures: a portrait of a woman with red hair; a still life of ingredients for a minestrone, tomatoes, onions, peppers and parsley with a yellow pot; and a seascape which I called Rocky Shore.

I packed them into a big case, chose enough clothes, hats, scarves and makeup to take me through a few weeks and a painter's smock. Then I said goodbye to friends and shut the studio down for the duration. Little did I think it would be four years before I reopened. In the meantime I would do not one, but four series of 13 programmes for British television, and two series in America for PBS. For each one, I visited dozens of towns doing promotions and though sometimes I was dog tired, I enjoyed it all. I loved being recognised in the streets and being asked for my autograph, invited to lunches and dinners, making celebrity appearances, all the trappings of telly "fame".

But back to the start. A car was waiting to pick me up at London airport and we drove to a small hotel called The Wilbraham in the heart of Chelsea, a 15-minute walk from the Thames where I was to stay for two weeks. This was my first visit to London but at this stage there was no time for sightseeing.

Peter Orton told me the programme-makers at HTV wanted a book to go with the series and it had to be ready in time for the first programme's screening. It was to be called Paint Along With Nancy like the series, and it had to show the 13 pictures with step-by-step instructions so that viewers could try painting themselves after seeing me on the screen.

I set up the easel in my hotel room and got down to work. I had a lot to do and using a palette knife rather than a brush meant the paint was thick so each picture took at least two weeks to dry. Then the instructions: exact measurements for mixing the colours as if they were ingredients for making a cake; three tonal values for each colour. It was a long, concentrated job, and it was not the only one.

Peter had been in touch with Daler Rowney, the suppliers of artists' materials who offered to make special painting kits for the series to include all the colours we would be using plus equipment like palette knives and canvases. The kits would go into bags with my signature on each one and Rowney's sold hundreds of them once the programmes had started. A few days after meeting the suppliers, I had an appointment with the editor of TV Times. He wanted to carry a cover-story about me and to run a painting competition for readers to tie in with the series.

At this point I was treading carefully, excited by the pace but unsure of what was going to happen next. Before the shooting could start I had to sign the contract in Bristol, then in the New Year, I was comfortably installed in a small hotel cum pub overlooking the waterside where I could hear the bells of St Mary's Redcliffe, not far from the television studios in Clifton. I felt excited but not nervous: and when I saw the set I was delighted by the ingenuity and imagination of the designers.

The room with the cameras was big, bright and hot with lights, with yards of trailing wires, but a corner had been sectioned off and made to look like the romantic idea of an artist's garret. Carpenters nailed up a piece of board to make the ceiling seem to slant down to a little window between a couple of mock beams and the corner was dressed up with a rickety wooden table covered in paint and half-squeezed tubes, colour-smeared rags and tins of turps and linseed oil.

A wide-brimmed hat, such as one would need against the Florentine sun was slung over a hook, and a big wooden easel where I was to do the demonstrating was stationed in front of the garret window with my palette. It looked the sort of ramshackle attic where a genius could paint his heart out, oblivious of the "simple" surroundings that suggested the scent of lavender, ripe black olives and yellow sunshine slanting over fields outside.

I set up my canvas and was ready to go. Twenty-five minutes to paint a picture from start to finish leaves little time for messing around. Verbally I dived into it.

"Just a minute." The red-haired director wearing earphones, who was guiding the two cameramen from a perch above them, wanted the script. He needed it to know when to go up close, when to change the angles.

"I haven't got a script," I told him. "I never have one when I give painting lessons. I just talk along. Don't think I could paint while trying to follow a script."

Very well, said the director, he would take the risk, but because I was not experienced in television work I should have a tried and tested performer sitting beside me in case I got stuck for words. The actor would put in a few questions like, "And what are you going to do now, Nancy?" to make sure there were no awkward gaps and his English voice would balance my American one. So that was how we began. I drew in a grid and four sunflower heads, and with a colour wash, started on the light and shade.

This two-person format was dropped from the subsequent series because so many viewers complained about the "interruptions", and thereafter I performed on my own.

When the filming had been done, there was the book to finish, colour charts to adjust, which meant frequent visits to the publishers in London, and promotional tours.

Although everything was now firmly on the rails we did not have a date for the screening. As an un-tried entity, "Paint Along" had to take its place in the queue and wait for a "slot" which as it turned out was not available till the beginning of the following year, 1975.

Meanwhile I went back to Rome, to the sunshine, the scent of fresh fruit and vegetables from the street market, and my friends who were eagerly waiting to hear what had happened. In my attic flat I painted more pictures ready for the promotions, worked out a grid plan for each and mixed the colours , making exact notes based on measurements by the teaspoon. When the publishers called, I flew to London for consultations, then back to Rome again. And as Christmas approached, I booked a ticket to California where I would meet my son and daughter and their respective partners.

My friends Louise and her husband James invited me to stay with them over the festivities at their house in Burbank and I accepted with alacrity. It was in Burbank that the whole painting adventure had started and I wanted to celebrate with friends who had given me so much encouragement when I'd badly needed it. Now in my triumph they were generous with their excitement at my success.

Louise gave a Christmas Eve party and many of our Toastmistress friends were invited. For the occasion I was wearing a long, black chiffon dress with the sort of zip at the back that needs someone else to do it up, and Louise was helping me.

"By the way," she said, "there's a mole in the middle of your back and I don't like the look of it. Does it give you any bother?"

"Not really. Throbs a bit sometimes," I said.

Louise had been a hospital lab. technician. "You must get someone to look at it," she said and as she sounded serious and reminded me next day, I took her advice and saw my former doctor in California. He said it should be taken out and I would need a few weeks of treatment. But there wasn't time for that because I had a promotional tour to do when I got back to London. So I said, "I'll see to it later."

"Don't leave it too long," he said.

Before flying back to London I spent a week with my sister Marie in Philadelphia: just time to see my mother and the town of my childhood—suddenly familiar again, yet now so distant—before departing.

I was back in London when, at the beginning of the year, the series started to go out across Britain at the rate of one programme a week over three months. Within weeks, the response surprised us all. Thousands of fan letters came in.

Viewers' enthusiasm gathered momentum, and the television company had to hire two clerks to deal with all the mail.

Promotional tours and book-signings were lined up. Peter Orton had been busy, leaving nothing undone, arranging interviews by newspaper and magazine journalists, painting demonstrations on local television, lunches, dinners, personal appearances .The TV Times painting competition had attracted a few thousand entries as well, and the pictures had to be judged and prizes awarded.

But there was something else. The mole on my back.

I explained to Peter, and he arranged an appointment for me with a Harley Street specialist. I am not sure what I expected, but it was not the cold, matter-of-fact verdict the specialist delivered; which was that I had a melanoma—a cancerous mole—and it required immediate surgery.

I was shocked. So was Peter. He faced losing his investment. I faced losing my life, or at least all my savings having surgery I could not afford in a country where I had no friends or family. I felt desolate and alone. In desperation I rang my friend and doctor in Rome, Dr. Stoppani, whose instant sympathy and help were balm to my spirit.

"Come back to Rome, Signora. I know a good cancer specialist. It won't cost so much here and you can stay in your own home with your friends around you."

I called Peter back and told him I was going home to Rome for the treatment and I could sense his relief. Weeping, I packed and left.

As soon as I arrived in Rome I contacted the doctor and was admitted into the Salvator Mundi Hospital run by a German order of nuns, one of the best hospitals in the city. After the operation, heavily bandaged because grafts had been taken from both hips to patch up my back, the surgeon told me that if I had waited two more months he could not have saved my life.

"Will it come back?" I asked.

"There's always the chance," he said, "but I'm pretty certain I've taken it all away."

As soon as I could, several days later, I went home and my dear friend Rolande who had helped me find my flat and my studio came from Paris and took care of me until I could move.

Mindful of the promotions tour due to start in February, I knew I had to get back to London quickly, and I was still heavily bandaged when I caught the flight to Heathrow airport. My Roman surgeon had been uneasy about the journey, but he agreed so long as I had a doctor in London to change the dressings.

Peter was relieved to see me and that I was on time. Literally hundreds of people were expecting to see me at public meetings and painting demonstrations; there were interviews arranged in major cities from London to Glasgow, the TV Times painting competition to judge (no mean task when there were over two thousand pictures to consider) then up to Aberdeen in northern Scotland and over to Belfast in Ireland. There were 13 cities to visit: 13 appearances at local commercial TV stations carrying my paints and easel with me. It would have been taxing for a fully fit person. But the excitement of it took over—the enthusiasm of all those strangers who wanted to paint; the trappings of recognition, and I was enjoying it again.

If it is cool for a celebrity to wear dark glasses and try to escape notice when "off duty", then I am just not cool because I had not worked this hard in order to be unrecognised. I loved meeting people. There is no rarity value to my autograph: I signed them by the hundred and was happy chatting to fans who came up to me in the street and in shops to talk.

Not that everybody admired what I was doing. In Glasgow, I was waylaid by a bearded man who, I suppose, thought of himself as a "proper" artist. He seemed rather angry. His whiskers quivered as he demanded sarcastically, "And how do you rate yourself as an artist, Mrs Kominsky?"

"Pretty ordinary," I said. "But I'm quite a good teacher." Nonplussed he muttered "sorry" and stomped off with his nose in the air. Against the handful of art-snobs who felt there was not enough suffering or "intellect" in my painting was the pleasure expressed by thousands who watched the programmes, started painting themselves, and sent the accompanying books into the best-seller lists.

This was at the height of the IRA terror bombings in Britain so trains were being evacuated and explosions kept people on the alert. The pub next to our hotel in Birmingham was bombed and when I flew to Belfast, security was so tight, all my paint tubes were squeezed, my painting knives taken and our cases sealed up. To top it all, the hotel I was staying in caught fire.

I awoke to loud banging on my door and the shout of "Fire". I shut my eyes to go back to sleep, but it grew louder, then I could smell smoke so I put on my coat, grabbed my purse and ran out. There was so much smoke by the stairs we had a job finding it, then we crawled down and a crowd of hotel guests emerged coughing with streaming eyes in the cold outside. I was glad of the coat. Beside me was a large woman in a very flimsy nightie. She must have been freezing. Two of the firemen undoing their hoses ran into each other, one breaking the other's arm, and in the midst of it all some of the hotel guests asked me for my autograph.

I was back on the 'plane next day for my next appearance in London, tired, the smell of smoke still hanging in my hair, but none the worse for it. In March Peter sent me a telegram to say that my book was fifth in the Sunday Times bestseller list.

It had not taken this long for HTV to realise they had success on their hands, and the result was three further series: in 1976, '77 and '78—and this time I did not have to wait for a slot for the screening. With each series there was a book. And running alongside each, another TV Times painting competition, the last of which brought in 10,000 entries. Although the actual filming only took a few weeks, the promotional tours took much longer.

Enthused by the success of the series in Britain, the American Public Broadcasting Service—PBS—bought the right to make 26 programmes, which were made in 1976 and networked, across the States.

Here as in Britain, promotional tours, television chat-show appearances, companion books and paint kits accompanied them. Looking back I see it as a time of frantic activity both in the UK and the States.

My US itinerary for June and July 1977 lists visits to Philadelphia, Boston, Washington, Atlanta, Memphis, New Orleans, Houston, St Louis, Minneapolis, Chicago, Milwaukee, Detroit, Phoenix, Denver, Los Angeles, San Francisco and Florida, finishing with a lecture in New York. And at each place there were multiple engagements: breakfasts, lunches, teas, interviews for Creative Craft Magazine, Associated Press, Better Homes and Gardens, Women's News Service, UPI, Brides Magazine.and many others

Broadcasting rights to Paint Along With Nancy were taken up in other countries.: Singapore, Malaysia, Arab-speaking Middle East, Iceland. .I had become a celebrity. Hundreds of people of all ages wrote from around the world to say I had started them painting, and exhausting though it was, I had a ball.

I remembered the times when as a child I had sat alone on the banks of the Schuykill river looking at the ships from unknown places and dreampt of travelling the world. Well I had done it. .Now after all these years of travelling and television I could go back to Italy and to the life there that had captivated me.

# Chapter 32

I reopened the studio in Rome and my old students came back. There were 55 now, most of them friends so I picked up on my social life in one of the most beautiful cities of the world where the skies are usually blue, the food delicious, and where exquisite architecture, paintings and music are part of daily life.

I loved being home again. Yet something was missing. Fame? I'd had that and the flavour lingered enough to satisfy me. No, I wanted something more fundamental.

I wanted some romance in my life. I wanted to share my life with a man.

It wasn't a matter of sex; it was, well, the whole thing. Male company is different. I didn't expect to marry a knight in shining armour or even to marry at all, but how lovely it would be to have someone special around who would think I was special, and we could do things together. I thought of Gabriel's plea to his love in Thomas Hardy's *Far from the Maddening Crowd* : "And at home by the fire, whenever you look up, there I shall be—and whenever I look up, there will be you."

Meantime, thank goodness I was in Rome and not in the US where not being part of a couple is a serious social handicap.

When one of my students, a (married) commander in the US Navy asked, over a cup of canteen coffee, "Why hasn't an attractive woman like you got a husband?" I stifled the retort, "Because they don't sell 'em in the supermarket," and instead muttered something about getting over the first one. Shortly after that he and his wife Isabella invited me to one of their smart cocktail parties and I went dressed up to the teeth in my best rhinestones, little black dress and my sharpest stiletto heels.

I was standing on the fringe of a group twirling a drink in my hand while Dan, our host proudly showed the paintings he had done in class, when an American voice at my elbow murmured, "I don't believe we've met."

I turned and saw a tall, dark, handsome man—the sort that Gipsy Rose Lee tells middle-aged women they are going to meet—standing beside me. His voice was pure charm, his smile could melt ice, and he had a wing of grey hair on each side of his head, which suited him so perfectly I wondered why all men didn't copy. In his late forties, I reckoned.

I glanced covertly at his left hand. No wedding ring! Most married American men wear wedding bands. No accompanying lady, either. He was saying, "I'm Commander Anderson. Jim," and he was paying me a lot of attention. I paid him a lot of attention back. We stayed together all the evening then he insisted on taking me home.

We walked across Piazza Navona hand in hand, had coffee at the Tre Scalini; we looked at the stars, the water splashing from Bernini's fountain, at each other's eyes, and laughed. Then he walked me to my apartment. I did not ask him up. We were decorous. He kissed my hand and asked me to dine with him tomorrow. "I know a marvellous Japanese restaurant. I'll pick you up at eight," he said.

I went up to my apartment, my heart fluttering like Madam Butterfly, cheeks glowing, eyes sparkling: I was ready and waiting next day. And the next.

It was a beautiful evening and a full moon, so perfect for lovers no novelist would dare write it. Jim's hand covered mine as we sat in the piazza. A couple walked by and stopped. "Hello Jim," said the woman. "How's your wife?"

Wife! His wife! When the couple had walked on I turned to Jim. He started to explain.

"I don't want to know," I said. "I've heard it all before." He walked home with me, apologising. "I'm sorry Nancy. I should have told you." At the door he took me in his arms and kissed me. I stood and watched him leave, then feeling flat and tired, I climbed the stairs.

Next time I'd be more careful. Meanwhile there were classes to take, and friends to meet.

I belonged to the American Women's Club in Rome and a group of us were going to Paris for a week in March for the Federation of American Women's Clubs Overseas (FAWCO) conference. It would include social events, sightseeing, seminars and lectures and at the end, a reception at the home of the American ambassador.

It was a stimulating week. One of the events was a splendid lunch at the Pavilion Dauphin in the Bois de Boulogne, during which I sat next to an elegant American woman called Martha Renaud who was married to a French banker. She was tall, striking (probably in her sixties, I thought) and friendly. I told her about my work in Rome and she told me she lived in a flat nearby with her husband and brother and would I call around?

The splendour of her apartment took me by surprise. It was surrounded by a terrace with a pale yellow canopy and standing there I saw a breath-taking view of Paris at my feet, fading into a mist in the distance. I was still gazing at it when Edwin came in.

"My brother," said Martha introducing him. I looked up at a well-built man, over six foot tall, with upright bearing and white hair cut short like a soldier's. He gave me a friendly smile, which I returned, and Martha told him about my studio in Rome. Then she added, "Edwin, why don't you take Nancy out to tea?"

Edwin took me to a little sidewalk cafe where we had tea and cakes and he told me he was a widower and his only son had died in the war. He was lonely, he said. He missed his wife of many years. When we went back to the apartment Martha said, "If you have any free afternoons, Edwin will show you around Paris, won't you Edwin? Her brother agreed with enthusiasm. Why did I have the notion his sister was matchmaking? I didn't mind; I liked him.

I had two free afternoons and spent them with Edwin. He drove me into the countryside and showed me a huge military cemetery, including a chapel, which he had designed. The hundreds of white crosses brought tears to my eyes. Edwin put his arm around me and led me out and we had tea in a country inn. He told me he had designed several military cemeteries in France, and that he had been gassed in the war.

Gassed in the war? With a shock I realised he meant the First World War. So he was older than he looked! More than 10 years older than me, I supposed. It did not really matter. I enjoyed his company. He came with me to the last cocktail party and buffet of the Conference looking handsome and distinguished in evening dress and I basked in the envious glances of members of the federated American women's clubs. It had been a marvellous week: some delightful dinners in private houses, special attention from the American ambassador and his wife who showed me their art collection, and now it was time to go home. Edwin did not try to hide his regret.

"Just when I've found you, you must leave," he said. "May I write to you?"

Martha was delighted that Edwin liked me. I was rather pleased as well.

Edwin had a chalet just outside Paris where he only stayed occasionally because he did not like being there alone. "I'd like you to see it," he said, "when we meet again."

I went home in a glow. Edwin wrote and his letters became increasingly warm as the months passed. He sent me his photograph and asked for mine. I looked forward to his letters and felt the initial attraction on both sides was turning into something more.

In August I had a letter from the chairman of FAWCO asking me if I could give a talk and painting demonstration to the club in Paris at the beginning of December. I accepted with alacrity, not least because it would give me a chance to see Edwin again.

This time, he took me to his chalet surrounded by tall fir trees, we dined out and I started to wonder what it would be like spending the rest of my life with him. It would be pleasant, I thought. And secure. All my life, from the hungry days with my mad mother, without money for warmth or food, the spectre of insecurity had followed me. What if I became ill again and could not work? Now this kind, attractive and financially secure man was asking me to be his wife. And yet, I hesitated.

"We would be happy together," Edwin said.

"I think we would," I said, taking his hand. "But please give me a little time to think. I'm going to America for Christmas but I will come back to Paris at Easter and I promise to give you an answer then.

He smiled and nodded. "Yes, it's a big decision. I will be waiting."

Back in Rome I packed for Philadelphia where I would stay with my sister and visit my mother but already I found I was missing Edwin. I received an affectionate letter from him, which made me miss him even more. He said he was experiencing his yearly bout of lung trouble, a result of being gassed all those years ago, nothing to worry about.

At the beginning of the New Year I had a letter from his sister. She said Edwin had died at the end of December, while I was away. Shocked and grieved, I put his letters in a box to keep and instead of the happy reunion in spring, I called on Martha to say goodbye.

Back in Rome, I picked up my brushes again. Maybe it was not my destiny to marry again. I had friends, and an interesting life and that should be enough. Occasionally I was

asked to make up the numbers at a party, which was how I came
to be at the opening of a smart new restaurant with my friends
Ned and his wife Joan, and the Brazilian ambassador whose
British wife was away in London.

The ambassador's residence was on the Piazza Navona so
Ned and Joan said they would pick him up first then come for
me. When they arrived both men got out of the car and Ned
introduced us. The ambassador, Jose, gave a slight bow and I
noticed he was tall, handsome, if a bit portly and probably in his
early fifties. I was glad I had put on my hot pink silk dress with a
short bolero.

When we got to the restaurant, Jose was uneasy about all
the photographers there. He averted his head: a picture of us
together while his wife was in London might not look good. But
after a good meal and much champagne the diplomatic reserve
melted, and before I could say "Ole" we were dancing a wild
tango. Jose waggled his fingers on each side of his head and
charged like a bull, while I took off my bolero and shook it like a
matador's cape and the other diners applauded. When we went
home at 3am we were like teenagers after a football match,
linking arms, and singing Granada much too loudly as we crossed
the deserted piazza. As we parted at my door, Jose bowed deeply
and kissed my hand. I stood there, as he walked away doing a
little flamenco dance as he went, stamping his feet and snapping
his fingers, then he rushed back, threw his arms around me and
kissed me. Ned and Joan were doubled up laughing when he
rejoined them and they went off singing. Next day I had two
dozen red roses with a card signed, "El Toro".

A few weeks later I was walking past the Brazilian
embassy when the doors opened and out stepped the ambassador,
beribboned, loaded with medals and looking very official. He
was flanked by an entourage as he stepped into a black limousine.
He did not see me and I smiled at the memory of the ambassador
who played hooky for one night.

I was almost, but not quite resigned to my single status
when I met the count. He was at the house of my South African

friend Berdine Audrey and her husband Robert the anthropologist and author of Territorial Imperative. The count was no oil painting, but he did look every inch an aristocrat if only because his clothes were impeccable and a bit out of date. He was sixty-ish, with a long face and teeth that stuck out and he spoke good English, acquired from an English nanny in his childhood.

We chatted about art and he told me he owned a fleet of Carrelli—the horse-drawn buggies tourists use for sightseeing in Rome. "I've never been in one of those," I said. After the party when the other guests had gone, Berdine said to me, "I could see the count hovering around you. He's looking for someone to keep him in the style he'd like to resume. Not much of his own left, I gather."

"I've learned to spot them," I said wryly. "But he won't call me. I'm not rich enough." But he did. He called Berdine first, and said he would like to go to the painting class with her, just to see it. "A reconnaissance," Berdine said. Then he asked me out to dinner and I said "yes" from curiosity and he picked me up in a horse and buggy, stopping outside my door with a row of cars stuck behind him in the narrow street unable to move and blasting their horns. Off we careered over the cobbles, swerving and jolting, the buggy filled with flowers, which as darkness fell, made it a romantic place from which to see Rome. The count, Giacomo, thought so too, and every time it looked as if he was going to grab my arm, I leaned over the edge of the carriage to exclaim over another ruin. In fact, I rather enjoyed the evening.

The count asked me out again a week later. It was his mother's birthday and he wanted me to have dinner with them at their Palazzo. Curiosity again made me say "yes". This time he arrived in a Fiat. He looked uncomfortable when he saw the white chrysanthemums I had bought his mother because, he explained, they are only for the dead in Italy, so I dumped them in his car.

When we got to the palazzo, we drove through a courtyard with a fountain and big plants at one end, old walls with ivy, all softly lit with lanterns. Up worn marble steps, we went through a dimly-lit hall with a huge ornate mirror and gilt chairs and into the salon, filled with antiques and paintings, more threadbare chairs, an empty carved marble fireplace, and a beautiful chandelier with just one light bulb in it. "For you, Signora, all the lights," said Giacomo, climbing on to a chair and screwing in more light bulbs.

The dowager Contessa entered and her son hurried across the room to kiss her, and introduce me. She looked at me coldly with dark piercing eyes that were the more startling because her face was so white and so was her hair. Her figure was plump, but she bore it haughtily, clad in black lace and pearls. I noticed her teeth stuck out like her son's.

We had dinner by candlelight, which flickered in huge mirrors with frames of carved fruit and flowers, throwing shadows across the splendid wall tapestries and twinkling on the crystal goblets, fine china and silver on the table. Dinner was served by an elderly maid in a housedress and slippers.

It was a strange and awkward meal because the Contessa spoke no English and I no Italian. I found the atmosphere constrained and oppressive, like going into a time warp where a secret past reached out and tried to drag one into it. I was relieved when it was time for Giacomo to drive me back, and I made excuses to avoid further invitations.

It is far worse, I reflected, being attached to the wrong man than being single, and as all my attempts to find the right man seemed to be doomed, I'd better snuff out my yearning for romance and just enjoy the friendships and social events that came my way.

Every day was busy. It was now the autumn of 1982 and my classes were thriving. Students came, and left when they were posted out of Rome but the figures stayed level. I had a telephone call one morning from a man with an English voice who said, "A friend of mine who is one of your students suggested I take up painting lessons. I can't draw a straight line though, I'd better warn you. Does that matter?"

Oh, that straight line! I've heard it a hundred times. I told him to come to the Tuesday morning class, and not to bother about straight lines. He said his friend Melanie would help him get the supplies. There was another man in the Tuesday class, a former captain in the British navy married to a French woman. The newcomer, Patrick Wodehouse, looked a bit like him: medium height, humorous blue eyes, glasses, grey hair and a moustache. The other man, Martin did not have the moustache and was thinner, but they were both charming and added some merriment to the class.

We started with a picture of a wild Scottish coast, which I called Approaching Storm. Patrick painted an unofficial abbey in the background where there should have been scrub and he was aghast when I took his palette knife and demolished it in one minute flat. "It took Cromwell years to do that," he protested. There was the usual light banter in class and I was sorry when Martin had to depart, leaving Patrick the only man in a roomful of women. Patrick did not mind.

He and I sometimes had lunch together in the YMCA restaurant after the lesson. We were relaxed and he was always amusing company but romance did not come into it.

When I knew him better I asked him why he had come to Rome, and he said it was to design the gyro platform of the Tornado military aircraft in 1972. When that job was over he stayed on working for the European Space Agency. His wife had died in Rome six years later after 31 years of happy marriage so now, he said, "I keep busy, but I don't like eating alone at home so I often take a book and go to a trattoria near my flat."

After a few months he said he had to go back to London. Only for a week.

It was to attend a celebratory dinner to mark the hundredth anniversary of the birth of P G Wodehouse, creator of Jeeves and Bertie Wooster and one of the Queen Mother's favourite writers. She was going to be there as guest of honour.

Patrick was PG's nephew (he used to stay with his "Uncle Plum" during the school holidays) so he was going to be a guest of honour as well.

When he came back, he told me all about the dinner, how charming the Queen Mother had been, how they had chatted about his famous uncle. Patrick's father Armine, was the writer's elder brother and following Wodehouse tradition had (after taking a double first in Oxford) gone with his young wife to India where he became a university professor. Patrick, their only child was sent home to England and boarding school at the age of four and hardly saw his parents again until he was 15.

The long parentless childhood didn't seem to have warped his character nor injured his sense of humour. He told me about school holidays spent in PG's big house opposite Hyde Park in London, with uniformed footmen, a butler, maids, and a cook below stairs who made the best rice pudding in the world; and Uncle Plum typing in his study upstairs, while Aunt Ethel did mildly eccentric things like washing the canary. (After a good soaping the bird flopped onto its back apparently dead, which made Aunt Ethel cry tears of remorse, but the canary revived and flew off).

The childhood he described could hardly have been more different from mine in Philadelphia, but by different routes we had come to the same place and we were comfortable together. Occasionally we went out to dinner; once we lunched at Patrick's penthouse apartment in Ostia, the silted-up port of ancient Rome. With a terrace all round, it had rooftop view across the town and inside it was cool, and clean thanks to a housekeeper who called in three times a week. As for being tidy—I'd never seen anything like this. There were wires everywhere, from stereos, speakers, light fittings, computers, ham radio, aerials. They came in through windows and doors, dangled from the ceilings, snaked along the floors and out of cupboards The study was like the workshop of a mad scientist, and the bedroom not much different. Patrick surveyed it with serene satisfaction. After all, it worked, which to him was what mattered.

We felt so relaxed together, I found myself enjoying his company more and more. By this time I had written eleven art books, most of them to go with the television programmes. However the last one was about mixing colours, like a dictionary of colour showing how to get 125 colours from a basic ten and it turned out to be the most successful, translated into several languages and published in New York and London. Before it went to press, I had to go back a few times to the publishers in London to make sure the colour charts were right. So when in class my friend Eleanor said she wanted to rent a little flat in London, I said I would go in with her and split the costs. It would be cheaper than paying hotel bills and more comfortable.

We were discussing the prospect when Patrick chipped in and said he had a two-bedroom furnished flat in central London that he wanted to let out. Would we be interested? Yes, we were! We agreed a rent and three months notice on both sides. It would not be empty for long. Eleanor planned to stay there in July with a friend from Houston, and I would go there a little earlier to do the book promotions.

Meanwhile I carried on teaching, dining out with Patrick, driving with him to little hilltop Italian villages in the evenings, exploring the ruins of ancient Rome.

One afternoon we went with Eleanor for a picnic among the Roman ruins of old Ostia. We walked down the ancient streets flanked on each side by the remains of merchants' booths, here the fishmonger's counter, there the wood-worker's shop, and the farrier's. Eleanor went ahead, out of sight—and suddenly Patrick flung his arms around me and kissed me. I was surprised. Exhilarated, I felt like a teenager getting a stolen kiss from her first boyfriend who may have grey hair and a moustache but was just as exciting. Eleanor came back into sight looking for us and Patrick quickly dropped his arms. But something had changed. I realised almost with surprise that the companionship, which I had so much enjoyed, was not just companionship any more.

Now there was no mistaking of our feelings for each other. Our evening drives were punctuated with "cuddle stops" and totally at ease and happy we knew we had each found new and unexpected love, and everything in the world seemed fresh and undiscovered and full of hope.

By now it was early summer and I had to go to London to deal with the book. Patrick had to go as well to set up the flat and to see his mother. Nell had been 20 years younger than her husband and widowed in her thirties, and now she lived alone in a flat near Wimbledon Common in south London.

I was about to book a flight when Patrick said, "I'm going to drive to London: cross Switzerland and France, and catch the ferry from Calais to Dover. How about coming with me? "

Would I drive across Europe with him? I could think of nothing nicer! I started packing. We left on a Sunday morning at 5am. The sun shone, the sky was blue, we stopped in a wooded lay-by near Florence for a picnic lunch, then drove on to Faido in Switzerland where Patrick had booked two rooms in a small hotel.

Everything was perfect: the weather, the countryside, and now we arrived at an hotel full of character and charm, surrounded by woods, a view of mountains, and at the front, a yard filled with flowers. The woman at the desk who was the owner took our passports with a smile and said in excellent English that she had reserved a room for us.

One room? Patrick started to explain that we needed two but he did not finish because I took his arm and whispered one would do. He smiled broadly and took the key.

Our night was like a romantic film, two unlikely stars to be sure, no Claudette Colbert and Clark Gable but who cared when it was so right and natural? In the morning we arose with delight to the new day and set off across the countryside, meadows jewelled with wild flowers, past sparkling villages and towns, Langres, Chaumont, St Dizier, Challon to Reims where we spent the night at an inn near the cathedral. It was like a honeymoon. And as happens when you are perfectly happy, everything went right. We caught the ferry to Dover and were in London by the following afternoon.

I stayed at the flat Eleanor and I rented and Patrick stayed with his mother. I visited them for dinner the next day. Despite her 82 years, Nell wore unbelievably high heels, and in her pearls and blue dress was a picture of elegance. Her sense of humour was as lively as her son's and I liked her. For the next two weeks I was busy meeting old friends, doing press interviews, talk shows, autographing books and then it was time for the drive back to Rome. The return was as happy as the outward journey had been and by the time I got back to my apartment by the piazza I knew I had met the man I would marry.

# Chapter 33

I closed my studio for good in June. The next year Patrick sold his flat in London. We decided to marry in the Campedolio, the Capitol of ancient Rome and now the municipal centre of modern Rome, but getting married was not to be so easy.

There were previous marriage certificates to be translated, and officially stamped, and the bureaucrats were too busy to do it. As a divorced Catholic I could not remarry in a Catholic church, so we went to the Anglican. The rector said 'no' because Patrick had not been a member for six months—though we could appeal to the bishop in Gibraltar. We decided to try England.

At the Wimbledon register office the registrar, Mrs Best examined Patrick's papers and his wife's death certificate, which was in Italian. She could not understand it. Nor my Californian divorce papers. We would have to go to the chief register office in London.

Sitting in the waiting room, we read Prince Charles's framed birth certificate and Charles Dickens's marriage certificate until the chief registrar came in. He glanced at the death certificate, which he could not read either and said, "No matter what language it's in, she's dead and that's that." He turned to my divorce papers and said he distrusted Californian divorces, but he would sanction our marriage certificate with a disclaimer, which would invalidate it if the documents proved to be false.

It was all we needed. We went back to the Wimbledon register office, a National Trust house with a garden in nearby Merton, showed Mrs Best our licence and feeling jubilant, got the gardener to take our photographs.

We were married on September 9th 1983 at 3.30. I wore a black and white dress in flowing chiffon with orchids and pearls and a hat with a short veil, Patrick's mother was in a red silk dress, tottering heels and a black veiled hat, my son Michael came over from California to give me away, Patrick's married son Nigel came with his three-year-old son, and a host of friends came from home and abroad.

Mrs Best conducted the ceremony but not quite fast enough for Patrick. As she told him to put the ring on my finger with the words, "With this ring I thee wed," she saw he had done it ahead of her. "Aah—not like thaaat, Paatrick" she said, each elongated "aaa" like the soft bleating of a lamb, "Take it off and do it again."

Nell closed her eyes; Michael stifled a laugh. Patrick obeyed.

"Now kiss the bride," Mrs Best commanded. Patrick did—with such enthusiasm my orchids fell off. Then he turned and gave Mrs Best a big kiss as well.

The reception was in Nell's sitting room, a bit crowded, but who cared. We were married! We had a one-night honeymoon in Brighton—the wind hurling down gusts of rain—but our real honeymoon was driving back to Rome, across Europe again, past vineyards, mountains, valleys mellow in the late summer sun, feeling the warm contentment of being together, and the peace of knowing what happiness lay ahead.

Five years later, in 1988, English Heritage decided to put a commemorative blue plaque on the house where P G Wodehouse had lived in London. Queen Elizabeth the Queen

Mother agreed to unveil it and Patrick and I were invited to the ceremony and the luncheon afterwards.

As she performed the ceremony, the Queen Mother said that whenever she felt depressed she would go to bed with a Wodehouse, "and I always fall asleep with a smile on my face."

"Ah", I thought, "but I go to bed with a Wodehouse every night, and I always wake up with a smile on my face."

# Postscript

In 1994 Nancy and Patrick sold their flat in Rome and came to live in Wimbledon, where they still are today. Nancy has outlived all her sisters and her first husband but she remains in constant touch with her two children who have stayed in America. She celebrated her ninetieth birthday in 2005 with a dinner for friends who came from the US, Italy and France as well as Britain for the occasion and the parties continued for far longer than one could reasonably expect. She still draws and paints.